BUILDING BLOCKS

ISAIAH 58 MOBILE TRAINING INSTITUTE

AGNES I NUMER   TERESA SKINNER
GORDON SKINNER   ANNELLA WHITEHEAD
KATHY VANZANDT

CONTENTS

Preface	ix
Introduction	xi
Building Blocks - Introduction	xiii
The Vision of Isaiah 58	1
1. Allowing God's Perfect Peace	15
Review: Allowing God's Perfect Peace	37
2. Attitude or Altitude	41
Review: Attitude or Altitude	49
3. Lord, You Have Ordained Peace for Us	53
Review: Lord, You Have Ordained Peace for Us	59
4. Spiritual Warfare	61
Review: Spiritual Warfare	85
Quiz: Spiritual Warfare	89
5. Conflict Revolution	93
Review: Conflict Revolution	103
6. Of No Reputation	109
Review: Of No Reputation	121
7. Shepherds and Sheep	123
Review: Shepherds and Sheep	131
8. Faith Worketh By Love	135
Review: Faith Worketh By Love	151
9. The Plumbline	155
Review: The Plumbline	167
10. The Vision Statement	171
Review: The Vision Statement	179
11. Praise and Worship	183
Review: Praise and Worship	191
12. Come Up Higher in His Love	195
Review: Come Up Higher In His Love	209
13. Where to Find a Word?	213
Review: Where to Find a Word?	221

Quiz: Where to Find a Word	223
14. Do They Know You?	227
Review: Do They Know You	233
Keys	237
Acknowledgments	247

Building Blocks
Isaiah 58 Mobile Training Institute
© 2016 All Nations International All rights reserved.
ISBN: 978-1-950123-31-5
Teresa Skinner Publishers

Unless otherwise indicated, all Scripture quotations are taken from the Holy Bible, King James Version - Public Domain. Scripture quotations marked (NLV) are taken from the Holy Bible, New Life version, copyright © Christian Literature International. Scripture quotations marked (ESV) ® Bible (The Holy Bible, English Standard Version®), © 2001 by Crossway, a publishing ministry of Good News Publishers. Used by permission. All rights reserved." Scripture quotations marked (Wuest) were taken from the New Testament and Expanded Translation by Kenneth S. Wuest © 1961 by the Wm. B. Eerdmans Publishing Co. Used by permission

Authors: Agnes I. Numer, Teresa Skinner,
Gordon Skinner, Annella Whitehead, Kathy Vanzandt

Special Thanks: Veronica Sanchez
Editors: Julie Montague, Ashley Flores, Nona Babich, Chastity Carvel, Amber Lawton, Melanie Rodriquez, Joe Rodriquez, Virginia Russell, Kathy Vanzandt, Linda Vasquez
Transcribers: Jennene Jeffrey, Kathy Vanzandt

Artwork: Adobe Stock
Cover Art: Julian Peter V. Arias and Eve Lorraine Rivers Trinidad

Isaiah 58 Mobile Training Institute
is available for use in training programs.

For more information or to
order additional copies of this manual:

email: is58mti@gmail.com
contact us: www.all-nations.org

We dedicate this manual:
To those who wanted to know... but never had a teacher.
To those who looked for the vision... so that they could run with it.
To those who want to know "What's Next?"
To those who knew they were teachers... but did not know what to teach.
To those who are looking for Christ in Us the Hope of Glory!
May this manual reveal to you Jesus Christ and
May the peace that He has ordained for you be with you always.

PREFACE

As we travel around the world, we see pastors and leaders struggle with, "What to teach their people." Maybe they have never had Bible School training... and may never be able to afford it.

Our cry is that God will read this to you... that He will impart His Gospel to your heart, that He will train you, and that you will experience the freedom, peace power and ability to demonstrate His Love to the Nations.

May we all work together while there is time.... That He alone may be glorified.

Let Jesus take you to the Nations.....

Teresa Skinner
    Director

"And this gospel of the kingdom shall be preached in all the world for a witness unto all nations; and then shall the end come." Matthew 24:14

INTRODUCTION

In 1954, God gave Rev. Agnes I. Numer the revelation of Isaiah 58. He told her, "This is My plan, for My church, for the end of time." He showed her planes, trains, warehouses, training centers, centers of refuge, food distribution and so much more.

Rev. Numer established training centers where leaders received a vision, a hope, a plan and the principles of God's Kingdom. Those leaders passionately put these principles into practice in ministries around the globe. God has been their Jehovah Jireh.

God also showed Rev. Agnes I. Numer a school of ministry that would share these principles of His Kingdom to the nations. The Isaiah 58 Mobile Training Institute is now available in print and eBook form.

Thank you.

All Nations International

> *Habakkuk 2:2 (KJV) "And the Lord answered me, and said, Write the vision, and make it plain*

> upon tables, that he may run that readeth it. 3 For the vision is yet for an appointed time, but at the end it shall speak, and not lie: though it tarry, wait for it; because it will surely come, it will not tarry."
>
> 2 Timothy 2:2 (KJV) "And the things that thou hast heard of me among many witnesses, the same commit thou to faithful men, who shall be able to teach others also."

Rev. Agnes I. Numer, also known as the *"Mother Teresa of America"* passed away July 17, 2010 at 95 years of age. She has leaves behind a tremendous legacy.

BUILDING BLOCKS - INTRODUCTION

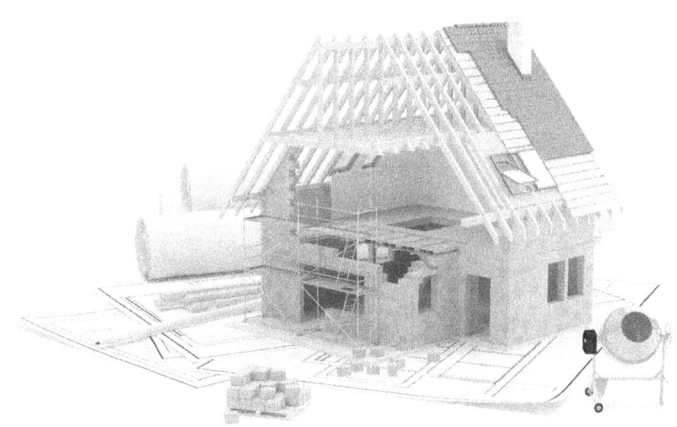

Demonstrate the Love of God.

How do we demonstrate the Love of God? How do we hear God's voice to know the needs of others? Inside we do not "feel" the Love of God. We have never experienced God's love for others. How do we get there from here? But we know that Jesus said, "By this shall all men know that ye are my disciples, if ye have love one to another." John 13:35.

These building blocks are keys that God has given to us through His word to guide us into His love flowing through us to the nations.

We must first become aware of His love and care for us. We must experience His creative miracles to us. We must become like Him and have His heart of Love replace our heart of stone.

Allow God's word to renew your heart, wash your mind and bring the revelation of His design for the nations as you read and pray through these **Building Blocks for His Life and Love Flowing through us to the Nations.**

THE VISION OF ISAIAH 58
AS GIVEN TO REV AGNES I NUMER

Isaiah 58

1 Cry aloud, spare not, lift up thy voice like a trumpet, and shew my people their transgression, and the house of Jacob their sins.
2 Yet they seek me daily, and delight to know my ways, as a nation that did righteousness, and forsook not the ordinance of their God: they ask of me the ordinances of justice; they take delight in approaching to God.
3 Wherefore have we fasted, say they, and thou seest not? wherefore have we afflicted our soul, and thou takest no knowledge? Behold, in the day of your fast ye find pleasure, and exact all your labours.
4 Behold, ye fast for strife and debate, and to smite with the fist of wickedness: ye shall not fast as ye do this day, to make your voice to be heard on high.

5 Is it such a fast that I have chosen? a day for a man to afflict his soul? is it to bow down his head as a bulrush, and to spread sackcloth and ashes under him? wilt thou call this a fast, and an acceptable day to the Lord?

6 Is not this the fast that I have chosen? to loose the bands of wickedness, to undo the heavy burdens, and to let the oppressed go free, and that ye break every yoke?

7 Is it not to deal thy bread to the hungry, and that thou bring the poor that are cast out to thy house? when thou seest the naked, that thou cover him; and that thou hide not thyself from thine own flesh?

8 Then shall thy light break forth as the morning, and thine health shall spring forth speedily: and thy righteousness shall go before thee; the glory of the Lord shall be thy reward.

9 Then shalt thou call, and the Lord shall answer; thou shalt cry, and he shall say, Here I am. If thou take away from the midst of thee the yoke, the putting forth of the finger, and speaking vanity;

10 And if thou draw out thy soul to the hungry, and satisfy the afflicted soul; then shall thy light rise in obscurity, and thy darkness be as the noon day:

11 And the Lord shall guide thee continually, and satisfy thy soul in drought, and make fat thy bones: and thou shalt be like a watered garden, and like a spring of water, whose waters fail not.

12 *And they that shall be of thee shall build the old waste places: thou shalt raise up the foundations of many generations; and thou shalt be called, The repairer of the breach, The restorer of paths to dwell in.*

13 *If thou turn away thy foot from the sabbath, from doing thy pleasure on my holy day; and call the sabbath a delight, the holy of the Lord, honourable; and shalt honour him, not doing thine own ways, nor finding thine own pleasure, nor speaking thine own words:*

14 *Then shalt thou delight thyself in the Lord; and I will cause thee to ride upon the high places of the earth, and feed thee with the heritage of Jacob thy father: for the mouth of the Lord hath spoken it.*

— ISAIAH 58

IN 1954, THE LORD ONE DAY GAVE ME REVELATION OF ISAIAH, chapter 58. And it was so mighty, I was very aware that it was by the Spirit of Revelation. I was washing dishes, it was Sunday morning, and I was asking the Lord a question. And that question was if it was His will for us to buy a house down in Sunland, Tujunga area. Now we were living in that area, but God was beginning to speak to me about coming to this area. He gave me a scripture, He said:

> *"Is it not yet a very little while, and Lebanon shall
> be turned into a fruitful field, and the fruitful
> field shall be esteemed as a forest?*
>
> — ISAIAH 29:17

I said, "Lord, but what does that have to do with what I asked you?" And He said, "Go and read... Isaiah 58."

As I dried my hands, and walked from my kitchen into the living room, and as I was walking through the room, all at once I was aware that something was happening to me. was aware that my mind was just moved out of the way, I felt a vastness as big as all outdoors, and I was aware it was the Spirit of Revelation.

He began, as I opened Isaiah 58, to reveal to me the plan of the last days, and He showed it to me in minute detail, every phase of it, in the natural and in the spiritual. He showed me His plan to help the nations. He showed me how He was going to feed the hungry, clothe the naked, and meet the needs of the people. And that in this hour, which I believe is now, that He is going to move very quickly, by the flow of His Spirit. He is going to cause people to flow together and do something that has never been done in the history of this world.

He showed me ministries flowing together as one, with one not trying to outdo the other. He showed me warehouses filed with new clothing. He showed me something very wonderful, that it would not be used clothing, everything would be new. The equipment would not be old worn-out equipment, but it would be new, and that which He was going to do was to go into the nations, and He is going to show them how He would do it. God is waiting for the nations of the earth to acknowledge Him, and when they acknowledge Him, He's going to pour out His blessings upon them. The devil is trying to prevent it, but I'm going to tell you this: In this day, they are not going to stop Him. This time it's not going to be defeated. He does it, man will not be able to say that they did it, because it will be so great that no man can claim the glory. God's going to receive the glory.

And these things which He's going to do are mighty. The people that He has prepared are waiting. And when He speaks the word, they are going to move in their place, and God is going to perform it.

He showed me how He was going to help the nations, to feed the hungry, to go in and teach the people themselves how to help the people. Missionaries have gone in, in the past, but for some reason the methods they've used has not caused the people to rise up and to learn for themselves. But God is going in with every provision, and as we teach the people in the natural and the spiritual, the spiritual and natural are going to flow together, and God is going to show them who He is. Now we have people all over the world who are trying to help, but God's plan is not going to fail. He just needs the people who are trained by His Spirit to do it the way He wants it done.

He also showed me the scientific things in the realm of the supernatural. And as things happen on the earth, He is going to take care of His people, supply their needs and they will supply the needs of others. We have had people ask us,

"How do you do this?" We say, "We don't do it, God does it all; all we do is flow by His Spirit."

We watch the Lord join us with people who know how to move by the Spirit of the Lord, and we know that there is a job that is going to be done. God is going to do something in our lives as we obey Hi. He said, "Our health would spring forth speedily and our light would be as the morning." But as we continue to move in obedience to the word of God and the Spirit of God, the light is going to get brighter and brighter. And then the Lord is going to say, "Here am I… what do you want? Here am I… what do you need?"

You see, as we move in obedience to the Lord, God will fulfill His promises. We've limited Him because we're afraid if we trust Him, He won't do it. Isn't that true? Too much to ask of the Lord.

One time when my husband and I were talking, I said to him, "I feel the Lord wants us to move to Antelope Valley." Then he came up and got a job; and the same day that he got a job, we passed by this house going to the fair. We had friends up here and we were with them. He looked over here and this was a beautiful alfalfa land. Everything was beautiful. And he said, "Honey, how would you like to live there?" You know what I said? I said "Oh! That is too much to ask." That's what I said. Next thing I knew he rented this place… and here we are. As I walked in the front door — I had not seen it, he had just rented it — and I saw the beauty of it, and I was astounded. And the other part of the duplex was not open, the Lord just opened it in my spirit, and showed me the whole house. As I saw the whole house, He spoke to my heart, and He said, "When the time comes for the work that I've called you to do, really comes, you're going to have the whole house. And that's exactly what He did.

So, God is faithful.

He showed me the ships, and He gave me the word concerning them. He showed me transport planes, and then He showed me all the provision which He was going to give, that we would have training places all over the world, so that the people could be trained by the Spirit of the Lord. And so, the Lord is doing exactly what He said, and we are seeing it come to pass. So that's why we're rejoicing this morning, because if God said it, He will do it ... and we can trust Him.

I'd like to read Isaiah 58. Now I don't teach just in Isaiah 58, but you see that's what God gave me to show me, what He's going to do in the whole world. So, I read it as it is coming to pass and rejoice in it and give God glory and not man. It's a wonderful thing to put our confidence in Him. And we know that He never fails, and regardless of what happens around us, we don't need to be afraid, because God has spoken it, and He will bring it to pass.

When the Lord brought me to the desert, He used me in a prophetic ministry, a very powerful ministry. But the time came when He said it's time to train others and to teach them by my Spirit. So, as the Lord changed it to bring to pass Isaiah 58, there are many things that are yet to come to pass. Part of it we're seeing come to pass, but I want to say to you this morning, God is shaking the church world today. He's shaking it because it must be shaken, and because He has trained us by His Spirit, we have to sound our voice like a trumpet and speak the word of the Lord. We can't hide, we can't! I remember when God gave this to me, when He gave me the revelation, the things that He showed me were such that I wanted to draw back, and I knew a lot of things that are going to happen, but I didn't really want to see it come to pass, because it was fearful.

And so God said to me, "There will be friends of yours that will drive up that driveway and I'll not allow you to give them food." That's a little frightening, isn't it? But He said, "I'll not let you do it, even though they are your friends, because their heart was not after me, but all they wanted was the loaves and the fishes. It's different if people don't have the light, but if they have the light, and they refuse to walk in that light, then God will not allow it. This Valley's had a lot of light down through the years and I tell you of a surety, God's going to shake it.

Because we've been faithful to Him, when He called me to this Valley, He said, "You'll not defend yourself…I'm your defender." He then said, "You go and speak my words to them and whether they hear or whether they don't hear, you speak to them anyway" (refer to Ezekiel 2:7). So, we did exactly what God called us to do. Many times, I wept before the Lord in this place, and I said, "God, how are you ever going to bring your body together, because you can't get two to agree?" He said, "What is that to thee…you follow me." And He said, "I will bring it to pass…" and he said again, "I'll bring it to pass by persecution."

So, we said, "all right, Lord, we're going to continue to intercede for the people." You can rest assured the persecution came. The Lord said to me, "It will not come (the persecution) through the world around you … it will come through Pentecostal people." And that's the truth.

So, we said, "all right, Lord, we're going to obey you anyway. We're going to speak your word. We are going to be obedient to that call and do what you called us to do." There's a lot of people trying to imitate it, but it can't be imitated, it has to be by the Spirit of the Lord.

In Isaiah 58, it's not what man said, it's what God said. It's what <u>He</u> is bringing to pass. We were told a few days ago that these people were all praying for us that this word would be destroyed, and they would take it up and they would do it the way God wanted it. But, you see, God spoke it to us, and it's God, that's brought it to pass, and it's a very dangerous thing to say, when you think you're going to destroy God's work.

I praise the Lord because God has a purpose for every one of our lives. And I praise Him because of the revelation of Himself that He gave to us that He is God, and there is nothing too hard for Him to do. And this which He is doing is beyond man's comprehension. No man is going to put a hand upon it, because God is bringing it to pass. I praise Him because that which He is going to do is far beyond what any human being can think, and that which He is going to bring to pass, no man can bring to pass.

> "For surely the Lord saith unto thee this day, this is the day of the Almighty. This is the day when I am going to show my strength, saith God. I shall not hold back any longer, but I shall uphold my servants, I shall show even the world

who I am. For yes, they have made light of me, saith God, but I shall laugh at them, saith the Lord. For they shall see the calamity come upon themselves, for they have mocked God. Yea, they have mocked His work, but I say unto thee, my children, I am the Lord and I fail not. And that which I purpose shall come to pass, and no man shall hinder. And it is so, that even as the light is come, the light shall be brighter and brighter until my glory shall fill the earth. And all men shall know that I am the Lord, for surely no man shall stop the Spirit of the Lord. For I shall bring to pass that which I have spoken.

For ye have not spoken it, but I have spoken it saith the Lord, and my word does not fail, but it comes to pass. For if you will follow me, saith God, surely you shall see the kingdom of God come forth, and you shall behold the greater works that man hath not yet seen. But if you will let me prepare your heart, if you will allow me to take from your life these things which have hindered thee, surely thou shalt see the glory of the Lord, and thou shall know the Lord thy God. And thou shalt surely know that the Lord is faithful unto thee. For I am faithful unto those that are faithful unto me, saith God. Be not afraid of the things that are coming upon the earth, but know of a surety the world is going to know that I am God, that I have heard the cry of the hungry and the cry of the needy, and I shall answer that cry.

So be unto Me that servant that I would have thee to be, and I will direct thee in all thy ways, and I shall lead thee into My ways, saith God. And know of a surety, the light shall be brighter and brighter and I shall walk with thee continually and I will fulfill My Word, and it shall come to pass even as I have spoken it.

Fear not man, but walk thou in the fear of the Lord, and know that the Lord is with thee to keep thee, to bless thee, to use thee that He might be glorified. For surely the Lord shall be glorified in that people who give Him the glory.

— PROPHESY GIVEN BY REV. AGNES NUMER

"For, behold, the Lord shall have a people, and yea that people shall be a holy people, a righteous people, and He shall bring forth His righteousness and His holiness through these people. And He shall speak His words, and He shall speak them quickly. And yea the truth shall come, and the truth shall make the people free. But if they hear not, the truth, they shall believe lies and they shall go down with the lies. For this is the day of revelation of Jesus Christ unto His people that cry out to know Him, for He shall surely reveal Himself unto them, and they shall know Him, and He shall speak through them words of life and not death…words of truth that will loose the captives and make them free.

Yea, this day the Lord is speaking unto thee, "look not about thee at the circumstances, but look unto the Lord." For surely the Lord shall take thy life and bring His righteousness into you…and his holiness. For yea shall have aholy people that shall be made holy by him, and his life shall flow through them, and the fear of the Lord shall come upon the people. For arise in His people and surely the Lord shall cause the people to know that He is God. Oh, man has thought little of God and thought they could do all things and get by with it, but I say unto you, this is the day when the Lord is taking His strength out of captivity and His glory out of the enemy's hands, and God shall be glorified in a people, and they shall glorify Him.

Surely the Lord looketh for that people and desireth to make every one of you that light that would be bright in this world of darkness.

Hear the word of the Lord this morning and hold not back, but hear the word of the Lord, for God would use thee, yea, in a mighty way, if you will let Him flow through you to accomplish His purpose.

Even this hour, saith the Lord, you shall begin to see the hand of God move in ways that you've never known. So be not in doubt and unbelief but give glory unto God and know that it is not man, but it is the Lord. Don't doubt in your heart but believe. If God said it, then God will perform it, for His Word is true and He is faithful and there is nothing too hard for Him to do.

So, yea, look unto the Lord with all thy heart and know that the Lord is there to help thee. Hold not back, but give glory unto God, and praise His name, and know of a surety God shall use thee to build up the waste places and use you to lay that foundation and restore places to dwell in.

The Lord shall give you the strength that you need, and He will cause you to do it, as you glorify Him, He shall be glorified, and He shall accomplish His purpose. Oh, if man would only believe. All things are possible to him that believeth. So hold not back, but rejoice in Him and He shall surely bring it to pass. Honor Him in all things. Praise Him in all things and give Him glory. And ye shall surely walk in the light of His presence. And He shall be unto thee that light that shall never fail. Thank you, Lord.

— SECOND PROPHESY GIVEN BY REV. AGNES NUMER

CHAPTER 1
ALLOWING GOD'S PERFECT PEACE

I. Introduction

THIS MORNING I felt the Lord wanted to share this scripture with you. This is a very basic scripture in our ministry down through the years, a part of our foundation that God has laid in our life. It is a part of our life: that we become as He is. And there are a lot of people having struggles right now, even in the midst of us, but there is a way that God has made for us that He will handle it for us if we'll give it to Him. If we keep it, then we're in trouble and we'll keep on believing lies, and the enemy will keep on tearing us up. But God has the answer in His Word because Jesus fulfilled it at the cross.

LET'S READ ISAIAH 26:1-15

1 In that day shall this song be sung in the land of Judah; We have a strong city; salvation will God appoint for walls and bulwarks.

2 Open ye the gates, that the righteous nation which keepeth the truth may enter in.

3 Thou wilt keep him in perfect peace, whose mind is stayed on thee: because he trusteth in thee.

4 Trust ye in the Lord for ever: for in the Lord Jehovah is everlasting strength:

5 For he bringeth down them that dwell on high; the lofty city, he layeth it low; he layeth it low, even to the ground; he bringeth it even to the dust.

6 The foot shall tread it down, even the feet of the poor, and the steps of the needy.

7 The way of the just is uprightness: thou, most upright, dost weigh the path of the just.

8 Yea, in the way of thy judgments, O Lord, have we waited for thee; the desire of our soul is to thy name, and to the remembrance of thee.

9 With my soul have I desired thee in the night; yea, with my spirit within me will I seek thee early: for when thy judgments are in the earth, the inhabitants of the world will learn righteousness.

10 Let favour be shewed to the wicked, yet will he not learn righteousness: in the land of uprightness will he deal unjustly, and will not behold the majesty of the Lord.

11 Lord, when thy hand is lifted up, they will not see: but they shall see, and be ashamed for their envy at the people; yea, the fire of thine enemies shall devour them.

12 Lord, thou wilt ordain peace for us: for thou also hast wrought all our works in us.

13 O Lord our God, other lords beside thee have had dominion over us: but by thee only will we make mention of thy name.

14 They are dead, they shall not live; they are deceased, they shall not rise: therefore hast thou visited and destroyed them, and made all their memory to perish.

15 Thou hast increased the nation, O Lord, thou hast increased the nation: thou art glorified: thou hadst removed it far unto all the ends of the earth.

Jesus paid the price there for us that we might take His Word and believe His Word and accept His Word. He said, "Heaven and earth shall pass away, but My word shall never pass away." This is how sure His Word is to us if we believe it. "And in that day shall this song be sung in the land of Judah." Now I call "that day" this day. I call it "this day". This is the day that He's going to do it for us. This is the day we're going to sing this song with Judah! He said "in the land of Judah ..." We're in the land of Judah, aren't we? Amen. "We have a strong city, salvation will God appoint for walls and bulwarks.

"Open ye the gates..." That's what we have to do. We have to open up to the Lord. "...that the righteous nation which keepeth the truth may enter in." Now this is a particular people. What kind of people? A righteous people. That what? Keepeth the truth.

Today you can hardly tell the truth anywhere. The Bible says truth was thrown in the streets. Justice was thrown in the streets. That's what is in this day. And this is the day He's talking about. "Open up the gates and let the righteous nation which keepeth the truth enter in." Now if we don't have the truth, we aren't going to be able to keep the truth, are we? I know a lot of people that are trying to fool around with God, and they want the things of the world, and they want to still be called Christians. That doesn't make us a Christian. What makes us a Christian is keeping the truth. Having Christ in our heart and in our life and doing what His Word says to do and to keep the truth.

II. "Thou Wilt Keep Him In Perfect Peace..."

"Thou wilt keep him in perfect peace, whose mind is stayed in Thee: because he trusteth in Thee." All right. If we keep the truth, if we are righteous, then we are going to be righteous in the righteousness of God. We do not have our own righteousness. You know we have plans. We say, "Well, this and this and this is what I'm going to do". Or "this and this is what I do and nobody's going to change me." "I'm going to do this, and this and this." And then you say you're Christian? Hmm...It isn't going to work. **The compromise that is in the world today is destroying the Christian.**

There's a parable, and it's called The Sower. And there's a verse in The Sower that says that some fell among briers and thorns and were choked. The cares of this life, the riches of this life, the pleasures of this life choked it, until it brought no fruit to perfection. That is the condition of the Christian church today. Why? How many of you worry? You worry. Why do you worry? The cares of this life. What happens when we have the cares of this life and we allow them to hinder us? We worry and we are not becoming fruitful.

What is the fruit that God is after in our life? "This righteous nation which keepeth the truth..." How many of you have perfect peace? You need this word. Amen. "Thou wilt keep him in perfect peace whose mind is stayed on Thee: because he trusteth in Thee." Why is it that we don't have perfect peace? Because our mind is not stayed on Him. Now you're going to say, "How can I keep my mind on the Lord all the time? I can't think about anything else." That's not what it says. Now I'm going to give you another scripture: "Trust ye in the Lord forever, for in the Lord Jehovah is everlasting strength: For He bringeth down them that dwell on high; and the lofty city, He layeth it low, He layeth it low, even to the ground; He bringeth it even to the dust...". Now who do we think we are that God's going to take away a whole city and make it dust. And we're going to stand before Him and declare "I'm going to do my thing my way"? Where do you think we're going to be? We're going to become dust, aren't we? We cannot do it. God has a better way. Amen. A perfect way. A way for our mind to be stayed in Him so we can have His perfect peace inside of us.

III. "The Inhabitants Of The World Will Learn Righteousness."

Now the next verse says: "Who's going to tread down the city? Even the feet of the poor and the steps of the needy." What are they trying to do today with the homeless, the poor, and the needy? A lot of them are on the streets. But what's going to happen to the city? It's going to be trodden down. It's going to go to dust. "The way of the just is uprightness: Thou, most upright, dost weigh the path of the just. Yea in the way of Thy judgment, O Lord, have we waited for Thee; the desire of our souls is to Thy name, and to the remembrance of Thee. With my soul I have desired Thee in the night: yea, with my spirit within me will I seek Thee early: for when Thy judgments are in the earth, the inhabitants of the world will learn righteousness."

Let's stop on this verse for a moment... "when Thy judgments are in the earth, the inhabitants of the world will learn righteousness." We, in this country, are trying to say there is no God, taking Him out of all our public life, trying to take Him out of our everything public. But He says, "when Thy judgments are in the earth, the inhabitants of the world will learn righteousness." Now God's judgments are in the earth. He's withheld it to His appointed time, but we're in that appointed time, believe me, when God is going to judge everything we do and say now. If we belong to Him, and if we want Him to be everything in our life, He cried out, "...with my spirit within me will I seek thee early." You know, people are afraid of God's judgments, but God's judgments are to destroy the works of Satan. Huh? God's judgment is not against man, it's against Satan and the works of Satan are in man. He wants to remove it and bring forth His righteousness in each and every one of us. He said the inhabitants of the world **will**, not maybe, not perhaps, but will learn what? Righteousness.

You see the world is in such disarray? It's determined to destroy righteousness, it's determined to destroy truth, it's determined to destroy justice and judgment. But God is determined by His Word that His judgment is coming first. And with His judgment is going to come righteousness. The inhabitants of the world will learn righteousness. How can it be done? God has a lot of ways of doing it. He has a lot of ways of doing it in our own life, a lot of ways of dealing with us because He wants all this junk out of us and He wants us to be pure in His righteousness and in His truth. They that are righteous and keepeth the truth. Now He's not leaving this up to us to change ourselves. He is asking us to let **Him** do it. He wants to do it, and when He does it, it's complete and it's thorough and it is perfect. Right?

Then He goes on to say, "...favor will be shewed to the wicked but they will not learn righteousness." Why? Because they are wicked. They want to know God. They don't want to believe that God runs this universe, and they're wicked, they're evil in everything; every part of their being is evil. And God is not doing this for them, because they will never become righteous. But they are going to see judgment and they are going to have to declare that God is doing it, even if they refuse to accept it, they're going to have to acknowledge it. "Let favor be shewed to the wicked, yet he will not learn righteousness; in the land of uprightness will he deal unjustly, and will not behold the majesty of the LORD." He will refuse, because in his wickedness he has no desire to know the Lord. "Lord, when Thy hand is lifted up, they will not see: but they shall see, and be ashamed for their envy at the people; yea, the fire of Thy enemies shall devour them." The last laugh is God's, because that wickedness that they're holding on to, God is going to send a fire and burn it up. But in burning it up, they are going to get burned up, because they refuse to acknowledge God and the Lord.

IV. "Lord, Thou Wilt Ordain Peace For Us..."

"Lord, Thou wilt ordain peace for us for Thou also has wrought all our works in us." What's He doing now? He's taking out the works of the flesh, He's taking out the works of the devil. He's taking out all of these things and He's putting His works in us. "...Thou has wrought..." What does that mean? What does the word "wrought" mean? Formed. He is forming us in His righteousness. He is putting His works within us. And sometimes, we don't feel that way. We feel all this other stuff. We wonder where His righteousness is, but He's doing something there. He's stirring it up so it can come to the surface, so He can skim it off. Amen... "Lord, Thou wilt ordain peace for us: for Thou also has wrought all our works in us." Not our works but His works. He's transforming us. "Be not conformed to this world but be ye transformed by the renewing of your mind."

So what is God doing here? "He will keep him in perfect peace whose mind is stayed on Thee." God's working with our mind right now. Amen. "O Lord our God, other lords beside Thee have had dominion over us: but by Thee only will we make mention of Thy name. They are dead, they shall not live; they are deceased, they shall not rise; therefore Thou has visited and destroyed them, and made all their memory to perish."

Let's go back. Other lords have had dominion over our lives. What a mess we've made of our lives. Because we did not choose righteousness. We did not choose truth. So what happened? All these other things came into our life to take charge of us. Our stories are many and varied of everyone in this place of our lives. But there is one thing that holds true: when Jesus is finished with us, and we allow Him to do this work in us, we're going to be righteous, and we're going to keep the truth, and we're going to have perfect peace.

He's talking about all these lords. Now we can make a long list of them, can't we? A long list of lords that trouble us all the time, and a lot of them are not even true. These lords come and visit us every day, they torment us, they lie to us, they just tell us all these things, and they are not even true. But they have dominion over us. Why do they have dominion over us? Because we have not given that dominion to God. We've kept it, and let it rule us, so that "...other lords beside Thee have had dominion over us."

"Oh, well, that's the way I am," I've heard people say. "If people are going to like me, they're going to like me the way I am...because that's just the way I am." And I look at them and feel sorry for them, because the Lord wants to change our life and make us like He is. God has a very definite plan to destroy those lords. But we have a decision to make. Now listen to it. "...Beside Thee, other lords have had dominion over us, but by Thee only, by the Lord only, will we make mention of Thy name." Only by the Lord is it going to be done.

But what? We have to let Him do it. "But by Thee only will we make mention of Thy name." We have to bring it to the Lord, and we have to bring it with a determination we're not going to take it back, that we want to be free from it. When we give it to Him this is what He does. He what? He says they're dead. So what happens? He destroys them. They shall not live. They are deceased. When they're deceased, they are dead and buried. "...Therefore Thou hast visited, and they shall not rise." If you're dead and buried, you're not going to rise. So He's made it so positive that there should not be one doubt in your mind at what He can do. Huh? "But by Thee only will we make mention of Thy name. They are dead, they shall not live. They are deceased, they shall not rise. Thou visited and destroyed them, and made all their memory to perish." Now that, we think, is the impossible part, huh? But if we give it to Him, and He destroys it all, then He has accomplished it, and made all their memory to perish.

"Thou hast increased the nation, O Lord, Thou hast increased the nation. Thou art glorified. Thou hast removed it far unto all the ends of the earth." I want to tell you today that I know the reality of this word, and there are a lot of people here who know the reality of this word. It's mighty, but it's up to us. It's up to us if we want to live like the devil, and we want the devil to rule us, and we want to be tormented day and night, and then say we're Christians. Not the Lord. Because He's made the way for us to have perfect peace. And it's not just peace that comes once in a while. "...will keep him, will keep us, in perfect peace."

I'll pray for you today, you'll have peace, and tomorrow you don't have it. No, He destroyed those things and buried them, and they aren't going to rise anymore.

V. Jesus Destroyed The "Old Man Of Sin"

You know, I was trained in a church that talked about sanctification. Then when I started reading the Word the way God gave it to me, I saw something different. They're talking about the old man of sin. Did you ever meet him? Did you ever know him? He's got a lot of Christians bewildered. Do you know what that means? I use to think that, well, it's your carnality that's showing. This used to be an expression in a church I was raised in. If you raised your voice or you said something that they didn't approve of, "Oh, that's your carnality showing!" I got news for you. **Jesus said He took it to the cross.** He forgave our sins through His shed blood. He destroyed Adam's sin in you, so what did He do? He took it to the cross. It was a curse placed there by the fall of man.

Jesus took it to the cross. When we are baptized in water, we have the privilege of carrying "the old man" down there and burying him. He'll let us carry that old man of sin... but He destroyed him on the cross, destroyed his power on the cross ...for every Christian, that will hear it and obey it. You go down into that water, a grave with the Lord, and you bury that old man there. He isn't alive when you go down. He's already dead, **he died at the cross.** But you have the privilege of burying him, so you know for sure he's not alive.

What a relief it was for me when God opened that scripture because I thought that all my life I was going to have to put up with that old man of sin and walk with Jesus. Thank God it isn't true! We might have a lot of things we need to get rid of, but we have Jesus and He'll get rid of it for us. Amen! He said it is so very important for us to be baptized in water, into Jesus Christ. Not into a church, not the Methodist church, not into the Baptist church, not into the Catholic Church, but into Jesus Christ. John's baptism was a baptism of repentance, but the baptism of Jesus is to bring us into Him. And He into us – making us into a quickened spirit. No longer of Adam's race, but a new creature – a new creation formed right there by Jesus Christ, as we go down to the cross and as we go down **into** the water. The old man is buried there, **never to rise again**, as long as we allow Jesus Christ to be the Lord and King in His kingdom in our life.

If we forsake Him, then we are going to go through hell. You're going to go through the horrible things that Satan has for you. But if you hold fast to the Lord and you do what He says, this mighty work that He has given to us is complete in Jesus Christ. "**In Him we live, we move, we have our being.**" He's the one who gives us perfect peace, and it stays with us. He ordained it for us. He made it possible for us. He made it possible for us to be baptized in water, as well, that we might be free from the old man of sin and that we might live in His peace to destroy all the affects of this life.

God has given us the answer - the New Birth.

He said to Nicodemus, "You must be born again – born of the Spirit, born of water." But here He is telling us how He will do the job. To finish what the enemy tries to make us think has to stay inside of us. God removes it... if we will let Him. If we don't let Him, we'll go on enjoying it.

I think some people enjoy it. I think **we need to get determined to let God take the junk, those former lords, out of our lives.** The enemy comes, and he'll try to say, "Now, look at you," if you make a mistake, if you get angry. Remember God made us like Himself. He gave us a nature like His nature. Adam gave that nature away, didn't he? But Jesus brought it back to us... if we want it. It has to be by our own choosing, whether we're free or whether we allow these lords to tear us up, day by day. Or will we allow God to take those former lords and totally destroy them and make their memory to perish, there is no memory left of them.

This Word is mighty and it is real and God is the one who perfects His people. Jesus perfected it at Calvary. He perfected it as He came up out of that grave. Today His judgment is still in the earth, and the inhabitants of the world will learn righteousness.

They will learn it through us. If we allow Him to finish that work in us then we will have His perfect peace. All these things will go from our lives and we rest in Him. He's the Lord of His Word. **It's up to us what we do with it.**

If we want to carry these things around and complain, it's up to us. What is so mighty is that He causes the memory of it all to perish. **We do not have to live with the "junk."** We do not have to put up with it, if we're willing to let God take it and destroy it. Amen. How much do we want of His peace? **He's ordained for us to have His peace. It's ours, if we want it.**

VI. "If We Walk In The Light As He Is In The Light..."

There's a scripture in 1 John, 1:7. "But if we walk in the light as He is in the light, we have fellowship one with another, and the blood of Jesus Christ His Son, cleanseth us from all sin." He cleanseth us. God Himself cleanseth us. If we make a mistake, if we sin, we come to Him, and we ask

Him to forgive us immediately, and God cleanseth us from all sin.

I believe if this truth were ministered in the churches as God intended it to be ministered, there would never be a backslider. Because when the devil comes, if we make one mistake or if we commit one little sin, he'll torment us until we commit a million. Then the devil has us hooked.

The Word says, "He cleanseth us." Jesus sits at the right hand of the Father ever making intercession for us as the Son of Man. He is still interceding for us to be free from sin, to be free from the powers of Satan. Here in Isaiah it tells the complete work. Here in John He says, "If we walk in the light, as He is in the light, we have fellowship…"

What happens? Somebody goes out here, and they commit a sin, and they come among the brethren. What happens? Oh, all at once they are not their brothers. That's right. You feel very strange among them. Why? Because you've stepped out of the light and the light in the brethren bothered you. **All you need to do is step back into the light and ask Jesus to forgive you.** Instantly He will forgive us, and then we're walking in the light again. And now we can join the brethren again and fellowship with them. Jesus says He has ordained peace for us. And that peace He gives to us.

When Jesus came back after He rose from the dead, the first thing He says to His disciples was, "Peace be with you." So the Lord is saying, "I've given you My peace." Why do you allow the enemy to take that peace from you?" If you've done something wrong, all you do is ask Him to forgive you and that peace returns to you. It's His peace that He's given to us. If we by our mouths and by our actions lose that peace, then we need to go back where we lost it and pick it up again. God has it for us, if we let Him give it to us. **But you can't keep a mixture.**

I am very much against some of the things that Christians allow in today's world, because it's compromise. And when it's compromise, you might as well tell Jesus "good-bye," because when you go over there, you're not going to meet with Him. No, you're not! You're not going to be with your compromise down here, with the wicked who refused – who refused to let Jesus give them perfect peace.

One of the very great signs of the presence of God is His peace. Jesus imparted it immediately to His disciples. When He came to see them after He arose from the dead, He gave them His peace. He's ordained peace for every one of us, and it's ours if we choose it. If we don't choose it, well, I already read what will happen to you. You go to the place of the wicked. The one thing I know, **God doesn't want a Christian to be tormented.** If you're tormented, you need to get rid of it. Give it to the Lord, and His peace will keep you. If you don't believe His Word, don't ask Him to do anything for you. He said to them that believe, all things are possible. He made it possible. He will do it for us but we have to be willing to let Him do it. **It's ours today if we want it.**

VII. Two Life-Changing Experiences

I had two experiences in my life. Two very, very important experiences in my life that changed my life completely and gave me His peace. I was being destroyed, not by my family, but by **what I thought.** You see, we don't have to be affected by what people say or do. **If we're affected by it, we are going to be hurt by it.**

My mother died when I was 11, with 5 younger brothers and sisters. My father never cooked, he didn't know anything about children, because he worked away from home most of the time. There were five younger brothers and sisters. Maybe you don't know what younger brothers and sisters do, especially if they don't have a mother and they have no one in charge of them. Well, they were going to give me a rough time. They said, "Who do you think you are? You can't tell us what to do." And what do you think developed inside of me? A lot of frustration and "junk".

Then, when I was 16 I gave my life to the Lord. That's when the war really started! The older brothers and sisters said, "She is a religious fanatic!" They took the children, and they took them to another part of the state, and I was not allowed to go and visit them, because I was a "religious fanatic". So they told all kinds of stories about me, and, of course, it always comes back to your ears. By this time I was allowing the effects of these things to destroy me. I had a call; I knew what God wanted me to do, but here was my family.

You see, it's wrong if we hold on to a family, when God is trying to separate us from that family, so He can do something in our lives. I didn't have any problem with God; I loved God. But I couldn't serve God because I had all this "stuff" inside of me. And so I was going down, down the other way, because I allowed things people said or did, or what the devil did to destroy me. This was not a joke, it was very serious.

One day the Lord got a hold of me and He told me to

give up my family. He said, "I have a family for you that's My family and they will be your family." That day I came about to the end of my life, and I knew it. I knew I couldn't go any longer and the Lord literally shook me. He shook me. He said, "I have asked you to give up that family, and you've not obeyed Me. Now I command you to do it." And when He commanded me to do it, I said, "Yes, Lord." I gave it up. I gave it up instantly and the Lord brought out every painful memory, everything that I thought was so horrible, I couldn't tell you what those horrible things were, because He took them and He destroyed them. But I had to let Him do it.

If anything is in our life that's preventing us from allowing Jesus to have full control of our life, we need to get rid of it. If it's a person or if it's things, we need to let go of them. Because I let go of the old family, today and down through the years God has given me a beautiful family – the family of God with all the little children I could love. My family – they are not my family anymore – they are just "kin-folks" that don't affect my life since Jesus took it away. But He had to take it away. If we hang on to things that God is saying to let go of it will take us and destroy us. But if we let go, He has something far better, **if we let Him do it.**

God has perfect peace for every one of us, if we'll let Him clean house and remove all the things that we still want to hold on to. It's very, very mighty what God will do in a few days. You see, God will do it for all of us. The reason many of us are still wandering around with our problems is because we haven't given them to Him.

Another time I was ministering in Northern California. I had ministered four times that day and I came to my room and gone to bed. The Lord came into my room and He started performing surgery on my skull. I felt Him open it up and I said to Him, "Lord, what are You doing?" I knew it was the Lord. It was as though I was visualizing what He was doing as He was doing it. I said, "Lord, what are You doing? He said, "I'm taking out what ought not to be there." Then I felt warmth, a very warm-like feeling go through my whole skull. I said, "What are You doing?" He said, "I'm putting My Spirit, My light there, and I'm removing all the darkness." And He sealed the place right here and He said, "I'm sealing that door, that none of these things will come back." It was a glorious experience, and it's never changed in my life since that day.

Those two experiences transformed my life because the Lord took out those things which the enemy would have used to destroy my life.

The Lord told me the conscious mind and the unconscious mind are like a tape recorder. The unconscious mind records everything that we see and hear from the time we are human beings. It's all recorded. All the "junk" you look at on television, all you use to hear on the radio, all the movies you go to, all of this stuff is recorded, right in here.

There's not much room left for you to use your brain, because it's all polluted. But the Lord said, He's the only one that can erase it, and He'll erase it from us... if we let Him. And that's what He did for me. He not only separated me from the people, He took the thought patterns so that I would not allow these things to affect my life. God changed my life so I could tolerate people, so I could live with people and so I could hear Him and obey Him.

God wants to do it for every one of us if we desire for

Him to change our life so that we can be an instrument of His love and His peace, His joy and His righteousness. It's up to us. I get troubled with our attitudes. **We're living beneath what God has given to us when we allow these things to affect us.** The Lord has the answer today in His Word: **if we want perfect peace, He will give it to us.** He'll take away the worry, take away the anxiety.

VIII. Conclusion And Prayer

I don't think there was a human being in the world who worried as bad as I did. That's right. From a little child I worried, all I had was worry.

I didn't have anything else. But, oh, how wonderful. **God loves us so much** He'd take a little old girl down there in Ohio, bare foot and not worth anything, full of worry and couldn't think straight and transform her life so that Jesus would give her peace. And He will give that peace to you. **His peace that doesn't pass away,** if we walk with Him. If we will let Him give His peace to us it increases in our life, it becomes stronger and stronger.

When I was raising my children I had a condition in my body that was very, very serious. My children, my daughter was 12 and my son was 15, had to put up with me, physically I was a nervous wreck.

And one day I went to a meeting, and I knew who this man was and I felt to go. As I walked into his meeting, he said to me, "Sister, the Lord is healing you now of a nervous disorder you have had all your life." It went like that, it was gone! From that day to this day I've never had it again. I had God's peace. I thank God for His love, for His peace, for His caring for us to set us free and keep us free by His peace. Amen. It's ours this day if we want it.

If you want to live with your problems, if you want to live with these things, then live with them, but God has deliverance for you. He has healing. He has peace. A very mighty peace **this day** if we want it.

It's up to us. "Lord, Thou hast ordained peace for us." Cause the memory of it all to perish. What a mighty God we serve. He's put it in our hands, and what are we going to do with it? Are we going to take heed and hear what He says and let Him change our life, or are we going to continue in the way we're going? I'll tell you one thing: I know you'll get worse and not better unless you allow Him to bring His peace and dwell in you. For God has ordained peace for us.

His peace – that we might live in His peace, walk in His peace, and become that righteous nation that keepeth the truth. Thank God for His Word. We don't need to interpret it. It is what He says it is. I like to give the Word and let the Spirit of the Lord do the talking about it.

Father, we praise You, Jesus, we ask You now to touch every person that hears this word. Jesus, whatever You gave us, You impart it to us. Lord, You know the need of every person, each one and everyone. You know their need this very moment and Lord, You have purposed for them to have peace. As they stand before You, that You look into every heart, every mind, every attitude, everything that is not like You. Jesus, I ask You to move in the midst of this people and set them free. Those who want to be free, Lord, I thank You. This Word You have sent to us. You have given it to us pure and undefiled and undiluted. You have given us the straight Word for us, this moment. Now, Lord, I ask You to search every heart, every mind, every person. I ask You now to work that work in each one that is willing to let You do it **that they might be free.** God, we ask You now to move in the midst of this people. In Jesus name, Amen.

LET'S REVIEW

REVIEW: ALLOWING GOD'S PERFECT PEACE

Fill in the blanks

1. "Open ye the gates that the _____ nation which keepeth the _____ may enter in."
2. "Thou wilt keep him in _____ _____ whose _____ is stayed on thee: because he _____ in thee."
3. "Trust ye in the Lord forever, for in the Lord Jehovah is everlasting _____."
4. "When thy _____ are in the earth, the inhabitants of the world will learn _____."
5. "Lord, thou wilt ordain _____ for us."
6. "Be not conformed to this world, but be ye _____ by the _____ of your mind."
7. "But if ye walk in the _____ as He is in the light, we have _____ one with another, and the blood of Jesus Christ _____ us from all sin."

True or False

1. ___ God's Word is the answer for all the struggle in our lives.
2. ___ What makes us a Christian is keeping the truth.
3. ___ Compromise is destroying Christians today.
4. ___ The reason we don't have perfect peace is because our minds are not stayed on Him.
5. ___ God's judgments are against man.
6. ___ Other lords came into our lives because we did not choose the truth.
7. ___ The "old man of sin" was a curse placed on us by the fall of man.
8. ___ "If we hold fast to the Lord, and do what He says, the mighty work that He has given to us is complete in Jesus Christ."
9. ___ "If we make a mistake, if we sin, we come to him, and we ask Him to forgive us immediately, and He cleanseth us from all sin."
10. ___ "If we, by our mouths and by our actions, lose that peace, then we need to go back where we lost it and pick it up again."
11. ___ If anything is in our life that's preventing us from allowing Jesus to have full control of our life, we need to get rid of it.
12. ___ The conscious mind and the unconscious mind are like a tape recorder.
13. ___ The Lord is the only one that can erase all we've filled our minds full of.
14. ___ God's judgments are to destroy the works of Satan.

Matching
   a. thrown in the streets
   b. Parable of the Sower
   c. Poor and needy
   d. tape recorder
   e. Jesus
   f. torment
   g. God's Word
   h. peace
   j. cares of this life
   i. "this" day
   k. curse
   l. new creature

1. ___ Where the truth went
2. ___ Condition of the Christian Church
3. ___ Who will tread down the city?
4. ___ Will get rid of former lords
5. ___ God does not want for Christians
6. ___ Conscious and unconscious mind
7. ___ The answer found here
8. ___ God ordained for us
9. ___ "that day"
10. ___ Causes worry
11. ___ Old man of sin
12. ___ Baptism makes us

CHAPTER 2
ATTITUDE OR ALTITUDE

Matthew 5 the Beatitudes

"W<small>HY DO</small> we have the Beatitudes? We have them because God is teaching us to have the right attitude. It is difficult for human beings to have the right attitude.

The only sure way that we could have the right attitudes is to have Jesus in us. Really it's not just Jesus in us, but it's His love that He must place in us. I can see a lot of flesh. I can see what we call human love. But it isn't sufficient to change our attitude. It takes God to change our attitudes. You might say, "You don't live around the people I live around. You don't know the people I know." There's one cure, that's Jesus.

Not half-way Jesus, but Jesus all the way. His love in everything! These are laws for us to live by. I used to think these scriptures were for us to get to heaven. No, they are for us to live by. Stop and consider our attitudes and see if we represent Jesus or if we represent our flesh. I've heard people say 'They have to like me. That's the way I am. If they don't like the way I am that's too bad. They have to face it.' We need to realize it is Jesus who changes our lives. We can do it anyway, we think we're doing it right but it shows up in our daily life and our attitudes. The way we speak to one another, the way we treat one another.

I want to introduce you to the real Jesus tonight. The Jesus Christ that God sent into the world because He so loved the world that He created – He wanted everyone in the world to know His son, Jesus. That still is the heart of the Father. We look at this world and it is all chaos. When God brings His judgment – it's worse than chaos.

What are we going to do? There's one thing that God requires of us – that we be like Jesus." Excerpt from message "God's Love" by Rev. Agnes I. Numer

> "One morning I woke up around 6 and went downstairs at 6:30. I saw Annella, who stayed the night with Agnes and told her I would stay with Rev. Agnes I Numer for the last half hour till 7. Agnes was sleeping and I noticed she had removed her oxygen. As I placed it back on her she woke up and started asking questions... as usual. I asked her if she would like for me to read the Bible to her, she said "Of course," of course.
>
> As I read the book of Matthew, we came to the 5th chapter. It was an unusual feeling to read Matthew 5 to the woman who spent years reading it to me. Pictures flooded into my mind of when Agnes would tell us to get the dictionary for the new words we would read in the Beatitudes. I remember it was one of the first lessons she ministered to us. God invests so much in us. Use the Beatitudes as a spiritual health check. I find areas where I

fall short and I ask God to bring the plumbline in those areas of my life, so that in the end, I may not have run the race in vain."

— TERESA SKINNER

Let's do a spiritual health check.

Read the scriptures below and answer the discussion questions.

Matthew 5:
1 And seeing the multitudes, he went up into a mountain: and when he was set, his disciples came unto him:
2 And he opened his mouth, and taught them, saying,
3 Blessed are the poor in spirit: for theirs is the kingdom of heaven.
4 Blessed are they that mourn: for they shall be comforted.
5 Blessed are the meek: for they shall inherit the earth.
6 Blessed are they which do hunger and thirst after righteousness: for they shall be filled.
7 Blessed are the merciful: for they shall obtain mercy.
8 Blessed are the pure in heart: for they shall see God.
9 Blessed are the peacemakers: for they shall be called the children of God.
10 Blessed are they which are persecuted for righteousness' sake: for theirs is the kingdom of heaven.
11 Blessed are ye, when men shall revile you, and persecute you, and shall say all manner of evil against you falsely, for my sake.

12 Rejoice and be exceeding glad: for great is your reward in heaven: for so persecuted they the prophets which were before you.
13 Ye are the salt of the earth: but if the salt have lost his savour, wherewith shall it be salted? it is thenceforth good for nothing, but to be cast out, and to be trodden under foot of men.
14 Ye are the light of the world. A city that is set on an hill cannot be hid.
15 Neither do men light a candle, and put it under a bushel, but on a candlestick; and it giveth light unto all that are in the house.
16 Let your light so shine before men, that they may see your good works, and glorify your Father which is in heaven.

What does the Dictionary say about these words in Matthew 5?

Poor in spirit
mourn
meek
righteousness
merciful
peacemakers
persecuted

Study and write the Greek meaning for these words

kingdom of heaven

comforted
inherit the earth
filled
obtain mercy
pure in heart
shall see God
children of God
righteousness' sake

How does this scripture apply to my "Attitudes"?

The Beatitudes say we are the light of the world – how do you see yourself as a light in this world?
How do you "giveth light" unto all that are in the house?
Read the scriptures below and answer the discussion questions.

Matthew 5:
17 Think not that I am come to destroy the law, or the prophets: I am not come to destroy, but to fulfil.
18 For verily I say unto you, Till heaven and earth pass, one jot or one tittle shall in no wise pass from the law, till all be fulfilled.
19 Whosoever therefore shall break one of these least commandments, and shall teach men so, he shall be called the least in the kingdom of heaven: but whosoever shall do and teach them, the same shall be called great in the kingdom of heaven.
20 For I say unto you, That except your righteousness shall

exceed the righteousness of the scribes and Pharisees, ye shall in no case enter into the kingdom of heaven.

21 Ye have heard that it was said of them of old time, Thou shalt not kill; and whosoever shall kill shall be in danger of the judgment:

22 But I say unto you, That whosoever is angry with his brother without a cause shall be in danger of the judgment: and whosoever shall say to his brother, Raca, shall be in danger of the council: but whosoever shall say, Thou fool, shall be in danger of hell fire.

23 Therefore if thou bring thy gift to the altar, and there rememberest that thy brother hath ought against thee;

24 Leave there thy gift before the altar, and go thy way; first be reconciled to thy brother, and then come and offer thy gift.

25 Agree with thine adversary quickly, whiles thou art in the way with him; lest at any time the adversary deliver thee to the judge, and the judge deliver thee to the officer, and thou be cast into prison.

26 Verily I say unto thee, Thou shalt by no means come out thence, till thou hast paid the uttermost farthing.

27 Ye have heard that it was said by them of old time, Thou shalt not commit adultery:

28 But I say unto you, That whosoever looketh on a woman to lust after her hath committed adultery with her already in his heart.

Did you know:

"Less than one out of every ten evangelical Christians maintained that adultery, gay sex, pornography, profanity, drunkenness and abortion are morally acceptable."

— BARNA RESEARCH, NOVEMBER 2003

To the church in Thyatira: "Notwithstanding I have a few things against thee, because thou sufferest that woman Jezebel, which calleth herself a prophetess, to teach and to seduce my servants to commit fornication, and to eat things sacrificed unto idols." Revelations 2:20

It's not so much about what everyone else does; it is more about what I do. How do the following scriptures show us this Biblical truth?

How do you and I both do and teach these commandments?

Read verse 27-28 Today is the day to check our hearts.

How do you see yourself helping your congregation to walk in holiness in these areas?

Sometimes we say a lot of things... do we say what we mean and mean what we say? Is what we say mean?

Mat 5:44 But I say unto you, love your enemies, bless them that curse you, do good to them that hate you, and pray for them which despitefully use you, and persecute you;

Today many hate us or are intolerant to us. How can we demonstrate the above verse in our daily lives?

Mat 5:46 For if ye love them which love you, what reward have ye?

Do not even the publicans the same?

How easy to forget…

Mat 5:47 And if ye salute your brethren only, what do ye more than others? do not even the publicans so?

How easy to forget… Especially if we think we are someone, a pastor, a leader...

Mat 5:48 Be ye therefore perfect, even as your Father which is in heaven is perfect.

How easy to forget our goal……..to be like Jesus in everything we do.

REVIEW: ATTITUDE OR ALTITUDE

1. Why did Jesus give us have the Beatitudes?
a. He wanted our lives to be difficult
b. God is teaching us to have the right attitude.
c. He wanted us to have more verses to memorize

2. It is difficult for human beings to have the right attitude.
a. T
b. F

3. What is the only sure way that we would have the right attitudes?
a. Study the Bible continually
b. Fast and discipline ourselves
c. Ask God for the Love of Jesus in our Hearts
d. All of these

4. Human love is enough to have the Beatitudes for all people.
a. T

b. F

5. To whom should we show the Love of God?
a. Our family members
b. Our friends
c. Our enemies
d. The people in our church who we do not know
e. All of the above

6. How does this scripture apply to my "Attitudes"?
a. It shows me how others need to treat me
b. It is not important
c. I am a leader and I don't need this scripture
d. It shows me where I need to change

7. How do you "giveth light" unto all that are in the house? (Choose at least 4)
a. I ask God how to love others
b. I tell others scriptures even when they don't want to hear them
c. I speak to others about things that concern them
d. I tell others about Jesus
e. I fight for my racial rights and privileges
f. I invite others to church
g. I convince others of my political views
h. I give groceries to those who have no food

8. "Notwithstanding I have a few things against thee, because thou sufferest that woman Jezebel, which calleth herself a prophetess, to _____ and to _____ _____

_____ to commit _____, and to eat things sacrificed unto idols." Revelations 2:20

9. The Beatitudes teach us to demonstrate the love of God to those who are intolerant to us in our daily lives.
a. T
b. F

CHAPTER 3
LORD, YOU HAVE ORDAINED PEACE FOR US

Isaiah 26:12 "Lord, thou wilt ordain peace for us: for thou also hast wrought all our works in us. 13 O Lord our God, other lords beside thee have had dominion over us: but by thee only will we make mention of thy name. 14 They are dead, they shall not live; they are deceased, they shall not rise: therefore hast thou visited and destroyed them, and made all their memory to perish."

"Lord, thou wilt ordain peace for us…" Why did he say it that way? He said it because He willed it, He desires it for us – but it is up to us to receive it. He said, "I will that you have peace." If He has ordained peace for us, then we have to receive that peace. He has also wrought – which is to beat out or shape all of our works in us… everything that we are He can make us.

It is not our will that gives us power to have peace - we can only have it if we can accept it. If we worry instead of accepting His peace then we will not have peace. Other lords rob us of that peace. Jesus said, "I give my peace to you" but if we do not receive it – how can we have it. If you have other lords in your life you will not have peace in your life.

Before we can have God's peace we have to clean house by acknowledging the other lords and then by renouncing them. "O Lord our God, other lords beside thee have had dominion over us: but by thee only will we make mention of thy name." We are not going to make mention of those other lords any more, we are going to renounce them we will formally declare that we have abandoned them. And then... we don't mention them anymore.

God said, "They are dead, they shall not live; they are deceased, they shall not rise: therefore hast thou visited and destroyed them, and made all their memory to perish." God took those former lords and destroyed them! If we will just allow Jesus to take those lords and destroy them God will cause their memory to perish – we will not remember the horrible things anymore. We will have His peace. He will change our life and gives us His peace. Jesus said to the storm "Peace be still." The Holy Spirit gave His Peace through the disciples when they ministered to the people. If the people received their word then peace remained. If the people rejected their word, then Jesus said, "You shake the dust off of your feet." (Matthew 10:13.14)

Jesus gives us this peace today. People must receive truth in order for their lives to change, if they reject the truth, they will not have peace anymore. If you lose your peace, ask yourself where you were when you lost it? What were you doing? What was God telling you to do? Go back to that place and find your peace again. God says, I give you my peace, not as the world gives. Let not your heart be troubled, put your trust in me, for I am the light of the world.

If you are out somewhere and you do not feel God's peace –stop and ask God what happened? Obey God, you do not want to be where God is not. We have to have perfect peace to move forward and do what God wants us to do. If we have both truth and deception – we have confusion. How are we going to know what we are supposed to do? How will we lead others?

Does the church realize we can be filled with His perfect peace? The world wants their way, but Jesus wants us to come to the light. If others reject the truth they will be deceived, but we will stand with boldness and we will have His perfect peace.

Sometimes when the devil speaks to us he tries to make us doubt; do not listen to him! Tell him, "You do not live in me anymore!" You do not need to argue with the devil, you do not need to be afraid. God's word is in us and He is the one that keeps us from fear. There is no law against truth, love and peace: no one and no law can take it from you. When we believe God's word then the devil cannot have any effect on us. Testing will come and that is when we must stand on God's word. He will use the testing to make us strong. When Jesus was tested He said, "It is written." He was victor over the enemy and so are we because we believe in His truth.

God ordained peace for us, He has taken us through, we have stood in the truth, and now God can use us to help someone else.

Oh Lord our God, only by thee will we make mention of thy name – the former lords are dead – if they are deceased, they are dead. If we try to dig up the past, we are digging up dead bodies. They are gone. As we allow God to take His perfect peace in us, **the former lords no longer live.** He ordained it, He desires it and He willed it for us. Whatever is in His will is yours – what are you going to do with it?

Where do we get the truth? From His word. How do you know you have the truth? Jesus said, "I am the way the truth and light." He is the Way back the Father. There is no other way. In the new birth **the Prince of Peace comes to live inside of us.** If we confesses our sin He will forgive us and give us His peace, His life, His love and fill us with His light. Then we realize our sins are gone and perfect peace is there. His written word must be strong in us! Jesus is the Living Word in us.

God wants to use you to help others. After He has brought this peace in your life. He wants to use you as a light in this world for others.

Discern the need that they have, the area of their life that does not have peace. Let them read Isaiah 26 and know that this is god's will for them. That Jesus died and rose again, that they may have peace and eternal life. Pray with them believing for this creative miracle in their mind, their emotions and their spirit. God will heal their brokenness and He will visit those areas of torment and bring peace. He will show them how to allow Him to make them into a man or woman of God. Show them to read His word and get to know him.

Encourage them to stay away and not go places or do things where those former lords had control.

This is something God does, **only God can bring this kind of peace,** peace that passes understanding. We cannot deliver someone from torment only He can. And when He does oh the glory! Oh the joy! We are set free.

God wills peace for you, He desires it for you... are you ready to receive His peace now?

Taken from the message "Isaiah 26" by Rev. Agnes I. Numer

REVIEW: LORD, YOU HAVE ORDAINED PEACE FOR US

1. We have the power to have peace by ourselves
a. T
b. F

2. God has made a way for us to have peace by:
a. Worrying about it
b. Trying harder to have it
c. Accepting the peace He offers us

3. To have peace we must get rid of other lords by:
a. Renouncing them
b. Giving them an official eviction notice
c. Wrestling with them until morning

4. In order for our life to change we must
a. Read more how to books
b. Often be defeated
c. Receive the truth

5. We do not need to be afraid of the devil because
a. We know his future judgement
b. God's word is in us and He is the one that keeps us from fear
c. We have a cross around our neck

6. Once God has taken us through, and we have the victory we can help someone else
a. T
b. F

7. Testing will come and make us weaker
a. T
b. F

8. The former Lords are dead, they are deceased and can no longer affect us unless
a. We sin in some way
b. We worship too long at one time
c. We dig up the past

9. We can help other people by letting them know God wants them to have peace
a. T
b. F

10. We can deliver someone from torment, and we can give them this peace
a. T
b. F

CHAPTER 4
SPIRITUAL WARFARE

SPIRITUAL WARFARE always sounds like something that we do. But it is God doing it through us, if God is not doing it, we should not be either. God came to set the captives free. He wants His people free more than we do.

During this study course look to Him for His divine guidance – who He wants to help and His compassion for the broken. Remember we only want to do what you see God doing. Also it is good that we do not try to do Spiritual Warfare alone, have someone with you who is a seasoned warrior.

The Battle is not ours, **it is God's**.

The Captain of the Host

Joshua 5:13-15 And it came to pass, when Joshua was by Jericho, that he lifted up his eyes and looked, and, behold, there stood a man over against him with his sword drawn in his hand: and Joshua went unto him, and said unto him, Art thou for us, or for our adversaries? 14 And he said, Nay; but as captain of the host of the LORD am I now come. And Joshua fell on his face to the earth, and did worship, and said unto him, What saith my lord unto his servant?6 15 And the captain of the LORD'S host said unto Joshua, Loose thy shoe from off thy foot; for the place whereon thou standest is holy. And Joshua did so.

God is not for us – we are for Him. In our daily lives look for the changes that God is interested in making. It is not how we want to change our friend or our spouse. When we are faced with a serious need for Spiritual Warfare, we remember that God loves that person more than we can – so much He sent His Son to die and live for them. We must allow God to fight the battle.

3 Keys to Spiritual Warfare:

Not by Might not by power but by His Spirit

Zechariah 4:6 Then he answered and spake unto me, saying, This is the word of the LORD unto Zerubbabel, saying, Not by might, nor by power, but by my spirit, saith the LORD of hosts.

Jesus did the thing He saw His Father do:

John 5:19 Then answered Jesus and said unto them, Verily, verily, I say unto you, The Son can do nothing of himself, but what he sees the Father do: for whatsoever things he does, these also does the Son likewise.

The blood of Jesus – paid it all.

One of the most drastic films of the battle that Jesus fought can be seen in the movie *Passion of Christ*. In all of the visual horror displayed; we see Christ flogged, beaten and hung on the cross, we must realize that the horror Jesus actually experienced was greater than could be shown through a movie.

Jesus paid the price to carry the authority over the devil. We only tap into and walk in His authority.

Let's Review - The Captain of the Host

The Warrior

God allows circumstances in our lives not to destroy us but to teach us and strengthen us.

Teach my hands to war - Psalms 18:34-40

For who is God, save the LORD? and who is a rock, save our God? 33 God is my strength and power: and he maketh my way perfect. 34 He maketh my feet like hinds' feet: and setteth me upon my high places. 35 He teacheth my hands to war; so that a bow of steel is broken by mine arms. 36 Thou hast also given me the shield of thy salvation: and thy gentleness hath made me great. 37 Thou hast enlarged my steps under me; so that my feet did not slip. 38 I have pursued mine enemies, and destroyed them; and turned not again until I had consumed them. 39 And I have consumed them, and wounded them, that they could not arise: yea, they are fallen under my feet. 40 For thou hast girded me with strength to battle: them that rose up against me hast thou subdued under me. Also see 2 Samuel 22:35.

A Psalm of David. 1 Blessed be the LORD my strength, which **teacheth my hands to war, and my fingers to fight**: 2 My goodness, and my fortress; my high tower, and my deliverer; my shield, and he in whom I trust; who subdueth my people under me. Psalm 144:1, 2

(For the weapons of our warfare are not carnal, but mighty through God to the pulling down of strong holds;) 2 Corinthians 10:4

People have said to me that they physically put on the armor of God every day. I tell them "I never take it off." Night time is a struggle for many people. The armor of God is the same as putting on the Lord Jesus Christ. You put Him on and do not take Him off. There are specific times that we refer to that armor – and recognize its use. Making sure our minds are protected and that we do not open doors through lying or other sins.

Armor of God

"10 Finally, my brethren, be strong in the Lord, and in the power of his might. 11 Put on the whole armour of God, that ye may be able to stand against the wiles of the devil. 12 For we wrestle not against flesh and blood, but against principalities, against powers, against the rulers of the darkness of this world, against spiritual wickedness in high places. 13 Wherefore take unto you the whole armour of God, that ye may be able to withstand in the evil day, and having done all, to stand. 14 Stand therefore, having your loins girt about with truth, and having on the breastplate of righteousness; 15 And your feet shod with the preparation of the gospel of peace; 16 Above all, taking the shield of faith, wherewith ye shall be able to quench all the fiery darts of the wicked. 17 And take the helmet of salvation, and the sword of the Spirit, which is the word of God: 18 Praying always with all prayer and supplication in the Spirit, and watching thereunto with all perseverance and supplication for all saints;" Ephesians 6:10-18

The battle is the Lord's – it is not ours.

If you went to an army base and used their weapons – it does not necessarily mean you are in the army. If you are in the army the first thing you declare is your allegiance to that country, government and officers who train and lead you. Just because people "prophesy, cast out devils and do wonderful works" does not mean that they are doing what God is showing them to do. It does not mean that they are being moved with compassion or in obedience to the King of Kings.

Matthew 7 "Cast out Devils" – I never knew you.

Not every one that saith unto me, Lord, Lord, shall enter into the kingdom of heaven; but he that doeth the will of my Father which is in heaven. 22 Many will say to me in that day, Lord, Lord, have we not prophesied in thy name? and in thy name have cast out devils? and in thy name done many wonderful works? 23 And then will I profess unto them, I never knew you: depart from me, ye that work iniquity. Matthew 7:21-23

God is training warriors for His Kingdom who will know who He is; follow His direction and who move with His Love. Then, when we meet Him, He will say welcome home my faithful servant. Turn with me to

II Chronicles 20

Jehoshaphat had a serious problem. The enemy was going to destroy his kingdom. Three armies – if you please, were headed his way with one idea in mind. Destruction! Let's see what steps Jehoshaphat took.

Jehoshaphat claimed a fast and sought the Lord

1 It came to pass after this also, [that] the children of Moab, and the children of Ammon, and with them [other] beside the Ammonites, came against Jehoshaphat to battle. 2 Then there came some that told Jehoshaphat, saying, There cometh a great multitude against thee from beyond the sea on this side Syria; and, behold, they [be] in Hazazontamar, which [is] Engedi. 3 And Jehoshaphat feared, and set himself to seek the LORD, and proclaimed a fast throughout all Judah.1 4 And Judah gathered themselves together, to ask [help] of the LORD: even out of all the cities of Judah they came to seek the LORD.

God's answer to Jehoshaphat

2 Chronicles 20:15 And he said, Hearken ye, all Judah, and ye inhabitants of Jerusalem, and thou king Jehoshaphat, Thus saith the LORD unto you, Be not afraid nor dismayed by reason of this great multitude; for the battle [is] not yours, but God's.

When God answered Jehoshaphat, he worshipped Him.

18 And Jehoshaphat bowed his head with [his] face to the ground: and all Judah and the inhabitants of Jerusalem fell before the LORD, worshipping the LORD. 19 And the Levites, of the children of the Kohathites, and of the children of the Korhites, stood up to praise the LORD God of Israel with a loud voice on high.

Jehoshaphat rose early in the morning and obeyed God

20 And they rose early in the morning, and went forth into the wilderness of Tekoa:

Jehoshaphat set singers and dancers in the front to praise God

21 And when he had consulted with the people, he appointed singers unto the LORD, and that should praise the beauty of holiness, as they went out before the army, and to say, Praise the LORD; for his mercy [endureth] for ever. 22 And when they began to sing and to praise, the LORD set ambushments against the children of Ammon, Moab, and mount Seir, which were come against Judah; and they were smitten

Jehoshaphat collected the spoil.

25 And when Jehoshaphat and his people came to take away the spoil of them, they found among them in abundance both riches with the dead bodies, and precious jewels, which they stripped off for themselves, more than they could carry away: and they were three days in gathering of the spoil, it was so much.

Jehoshaphat took special care to thank God for His intervention.

26 And on the fourth day they assembled themselves in the valley of Berachah; for there they blessed the LORD: therefore the name of the same place was called, The valley of Berachah, unto this day. 27 Then they returned, every man of Judah and Jerusalem, and Jehoshaphat in the forefront of them, to go again to Jerusalem with joy; for the LORD had made them to rejoice over their enemies. 28 And they came to Jerusalem with psalteries and harps and trumpets unto the house of the LORD. 29 And the fear of God was on all the kingdoms of [those] countries, when they had heard that the LORD fought against the enemies of Israel.

God's presence – your refuge – your Key
More Keys:

- You cannot impart what you don't have
- If God has not given you direction – do not move in presumption.
- No Fear – do not give place to fear
- Do not focus on the enemy.

Focus on what is God doing and saying – right now. What is this person's greatest need? "God how should we pray in this circumstance? What is your direction?" Do not give place to worry and fear. Search the Word of God to know what His word says about the situation.

Although we are seeking and waiting upon God for His direction it does not mean that we do nothing – if you need a job, get up early in the morning and pray, clean yourself up and go look for a job. In the military the soldier prepares his weapons and waits for his orders. Do what you know you should do and also wait upon God.

Warfare in music – What did Jehoshaphat do?

Praise and worship is an important key. God inhabits the praises of His people and when we are ministering to someone or battling for our own lives we need His presence. Praise ministers to God and ministers to us as well.

Go 2 x 2

When praying deliverance for someone, counseling, or ministering to them – take someone with you. If you get into the position where you must minister or counsel someone of the opposite sex keep your heart before God and take someone with you. Do not become so emotionally involved with them that you miss helping them. It is best that men minister to men and women to women.

And he called [unto him] the twelve, and began to send them forth by two and two; and gave them power over unclean spirits Matthew 6:7

Don't cast out in Anger, Arrogance or Pride

You cannot cast out sin with sin. Anger, Arrogance and Pride is sin.

Just because it irritates you does not mean it is a spirit or that it bothers God.

I have heard of people saying "I bind you in the name of Jesus" as they are speaking to their spouse or friend because that person is not doing what they want. This is not about us! It is about the Love of God being demonstrated to the world, so that they may know Him! Are we praying and fasting for our own selfish needs or for their salvation?

Guard your heart

People's emotions are so high during these times, we must keep focused that this is not about us, it is about **God's pure love being demonstrated** to this person, that they may be healed and restored to wholeness.

Keep thy heart with all diligence; for out of it [are] the issues of life. Proverbs 4:23

Wherefore let him that thinketh he standeth take heed lest he fall. I Corinthians 10:12

A bird may fly over but don't let them nest on your head.

Thoughts, thoughts, thoughts... Once we are free and as well as when we are working with others, a thought that comes to your mind does not mean that it is "the devil" or that we are defeated. When wrong thoughts come, **do not take them and dwell on them.** Neither do we need to condemn ourselves because a thought came into our mind.

He will change our lives and our minds as we seek Him and let Him.

Then will I sprinkle clean water upon you, and ye shall be clean: from all your filthiness, and from all your idols, will I cleanse you. Ezekiel 36:25

That he might sanctify and cleanse it with the washing of water by the word, 27 That he might present it to himself a glorious church, not having spot, or wrinkle, or any such thing; but that it should be holy and without blemish. Ephesians 5:26-27

Let's Review - The Warrior

The Enemy

Jesus I know, Paul I know, but who are you?

And the evil spirit answered and said, Jesus I know, and Paul I know; but who are ye? Acts 19:15

God's enemy is strong and powerful; he is not to be played with.

How art thou fallen from heaven, O Lucifer, son of the morning! [how] art thou cut down to the ground, which didst weaken the nations! Isaiah 14:12

The enemy hates God. He hates us because we were formed in God's image and we remind him of God.

And the LORD God said unto the serpent, Because thou hast done this, thou [art] cursed above all cattle, and above every beast of the field; upon thy belly shalt thou go, and dust shalt thou eat all the days of thy life: 15 And I will put enmity between thee and the woman, and between thy seed and her seed; it shall bruise thy head, and thou shalt bruise his heel. Genesis 3:14, 15

Carnal Nature: Everything we were before Christ, everything we inherited from Adam, everything that functions on the DNA of Adam.

Our carnal nature – no matter how we dress it or disguise it has no power when it comes to spiritual things. And it has no power over God's enemy. Our Hope and Strength is:

Jesus paid the price to carry the authority over the devil.

We tap into and walk in His authority.

3 For though we walk in the flesh, we do not war after the flesh: 4 (For the weapons of our warfare [are] not carnal, but mighty through God to the pulling down of strong holds;) 5 Casting down imaginations, and every high thing that exalteth itself against the knowledge of God, and bringing into captivity every thought to the obedience of Christ; II Corinthians 10:3-5

Don't give place to the devil

Spiritual Warfare is carried out through the authority of Jesus Christ. We cannot cast out sin with sin. This scripture tells us how not to give place to the devil:

22 That ye put off concerning the former conversation the old man, which is corrupt according to the deceitful lusts; 23 And be renewed in the spirit of your mind; 24 And that ye put on the new man, which after God is created in righteousness and true holiness. 25 Wherefore putting away lying, speak every man truth with his neighbour: for we are members one of another. 26 Be ye angry, and sin not: let not the sun go down upon your wrath: 27 Neither give place to

the devil. 28 Let him that stole steal no more: but rather let him labour, working with [his] hands the thing which is good, that he may have to give to him that needeth. 29 Let no corrupt communication proceed out of your mouth, but that which is good to the use of edifying, that it may minister grace unto the hearers. 30 And grieve not the Holy Spirit of God, whereby ye are sealed unto the day of redemption. 31 Let all bitterness, and wrath, and anger, and clamour, and evil speaking, be put away from you, with all malice: 32 And be ye kind one to another, tenderhearted, forgiving one another, even as God for Christ's sake hath forgiven you. Ephesians 4:22-32

The Enemy's weapon of division:

When we train ministers and Pastors overseas one of the first questions that comes up was why was it that when they went on the Mission field to a dark place they always ended up fighting with each other. God commands a blessing when there is unity. God's enemy enjoys division – one of the greatest war tactics is to cause division in the enemy's camp – cause them to fight amongst themselves.

When we feel this presence of Division pray against it and **allow God's love to flow** through us for each other and refuse to react to flesh with our flesh.

Armor of Christ

13 Wherefore take unto you the whole armor of God, that ye may be able to withstand in the evil day, and having done all, to stand. 14 Stand therefore, having your loins girt about with truth, and having on the breastplate of righteousness; 15 And your feet shod with the preparation of the gospel of peace; 16 Above all, taking the shield of faith, wherewith ye shall be able to quench all the fiery darts

of the wicked. 17 And take the helmet of salvation, and the sword of the Spirit, which is the word of God: 18 Praying always with all prayer and supplication in the Spirit, and watching thereunto with all perseverance and supplication for all saints; Ephesians 6:13-18

14 But put ye on the Lord Jesus Christ, and make not provision for the flesh, to [fulfil] the lusts [thereof]. Romans 13:14

Notice how the Armor of Christ is covered when **we put on the Lord Jesus Christ?** Our head is covered with His Salvation, Water Baptism dissolves the Adamic Nature. When we walk in His Spirit we cover our most life giving areas with Truth and Righteousness?

When we put on the Lord Jesus Christ and make no provision for the flesh – we live with His Armor.

The enemy hates God. He hates us because we were formed in God's image and we remind him of God. We do not trust the enemy or what he says. When we see him we ask "Lord what do You want me to do about this situation." We begin praying for the person and seeking God for the person's salvation. Then when it is time to pray, we bind those powers to the pit of hell in the name of Jesus Christ. We pray by the authority of the One who paid the price.

Excerpt from "Intercession" by Rev. Agnes I. Numer

Read Daniel chapter 10.

Daniel started to pray and God heard it from the moment he set His heart toward God. He heard and knew the cry of Daniel's heart. But the powers, the principalities in the air that stood prevented that prayer from coming through to God. And the whole thing as Daniel was praying the Lord was revealing himself to Daniel. It was Christ that Daniel saw and that ministered to him. But he said that it took that long 21 days to break through the principalities and powers that were in the air and Daniel knew that God heard his prayer but he couldn't bring the answer back until he did the spiritual warfare in the heavens.

I know the powers of Satan are heavier over some cities than others. These are powers that the enemy has set over areas to linger there. So Daniel didn't eat. I think he must have fasted those 21 days. But the Lord wanted him to know that the moment he set his heart to pray – God heard his prayer.

I know this is true. God has given us such a mighty thing and we are blessed with the Holy Ghost as well. We're blessed with One that takes that prayer and takes it to the Father according to the will of God. We're blessed today even though the principalities were cast down to the earth. Now, Satan can't go into the heavens to declare things against us to the Father. That thing is broken. God has given us authority and dominion to pull down the powers and principalities through prayer and intercession.

Let's Review - The Enemy

The Captive

The Captive in this section can be any person, your neighbor, the person on the street, your family; even you can be a captive.

God never intended for us to be captives.

But unto every one of us is given grace according to the measure of the gift of Christ. 8 Wherefore he saith, When he ascended up on high, he led captivity captive, and gave gifts unto men Ephesians 4:7, 8

18 The Spirit of the Lord [is] upon me, because he hath anointed me to preach the gospel to the poor; he hath sent me to heal the brokenhearted, to preach deliverance to the captives, and recovering of sight to the blind, to set at liberty them that are bruised, 19 To preach the acceptable year of the Lord. Luke 4:18, 19

From before the fall of the first Adam, God had a plan to restore His people back to Himself.

Let no man say when he is tempted, I am tempted of God: for God cannot be tempted with evil, neither tempteth he any man:4 14 But every man is tempted, when he is drawn away of his own lust, and enticed. 15 Then when lust hath conceived, it bringeth forth sin: and sin, when it is finished, bringeth forth death. James 1: 13-15

Know the LORD: for they shall all know me, from the least of them unto the greatest of them, saith the LORD: for I will forgive their iniquity, and I will remember their sin no more. Jeremiah 31.34

God's Heart is continually moved with compassion for His people that they may truly embrace His nature – His DNA and live with His peace.

LORD, thou wilt ordain peace for us: for thou also hast wrought all our works in us.6 13 O LORD our God, [other] lords beside thee have had dominion over us: [but] by thee only will we make mention of thy name. 14 [They are] dead, they shall not live; [they are] deceased, they shall not rise: therefore hast thou visited and destroyed them, and made all their memory to perish. Isaiah 26:12-14

In our lives God does not just want to destroy the enemy

but to cause even the enemy's memory to perish! This is God's plan! Many captives do not realize God wants them to have peace.

Jesus cast out a devil that was dumb or as we say today mute – the person could not speak. When he was finished people wondered how this could be. I can imagine the fear and bewilderment – this deliverance was something no one had seen during Jesus' day. And then, Jesus took that opportunity to teach a lesson on spiritual warfare to those that had an ear to hear:

When the unclean spirit is gone out of a man, he walketh through dry places, seeking rest; and finding none, he saith, I will return unto my house whence I came out. 25 And when he cometh, he findeth [it] swept and garnished. 26 Then goeth he, and taketh [to him] seven other spirits more wicked than himself; and they enter in, and dwell there: and the last [state] of that man is worse than the first. Like 11:24-26

Excerpt from "Full Redemption" by Rev. Agnes I. Numer:

"Jesus didn't go through the crucifixion just to do a half way job. He did a perfect work – it's we that do a half way job. God's not going to let us get by with a halfway job, I let you know that. We have to allow Him to clean our whole house. God gave me a vision one time of a mansion. It was a beautiful mansion but it was filthy. He said this is the way you were to me. He said I bought you as you were now I'm going to clean you up. You are like this mansion: cob webs, black walls, filth all over the place and then the Lord said I'm going to rejuvenate you and I'm going to change you.

See if we let Him do it – we say I love you and I will let you clean my house – but the other rooms are locked!

That's the way we want to serve the Lord but that isn't the way we should serve the Lord. We either have to open the whole house to Him or He won't take any of it. What if you bought a house and the former owner wants to live in that house – you pay for a whole house and he keeps 3/4th of it? I don't think that's going to work. It's the same way with Jesus – we can't half way serve Him. We have to come with all our heart, with all our soul, mind, and strength – body, mind and soul. Jesus paid that price."

Seven times worse is no game – it is nothing to play with.

When God delivers someone and their "house" is swept clean what do they do? How do they fill their "house?"

Then goeth he, and taketh [to him] seven other spirits more wicked than himself; and they enter in, and dwell there: and the last [state] of that man is worse than the first. Luke 11:26

After deliverance people can feel empty and a bit lost. The former lord of that area in their life is gone and now what do they do? These areas need to be filled with God! Pray for God to fill the person with His Peace and His Joy. If they are not born again, teach them about Salvation and ask them if they would ask Jesus into their heart. Lead them to the next level in their walk with God. Teach them how to close doors that they opened to the enemy. Encourage them to go to church and fellowship with those who will minister strength and healing to them.

Jesus saith unto him, Rise, take up thy bed, and walk. 9 And immediately the man was made whole, and took up his bed, and walked: and on the same day was the sabbath.... 14 Afterward Jesus findeth him in the temple, and said unto him, Behold, thou art made whole: sin no more, lest a worse thing come unto thee. John 5:8, 14

When Jesus had lifted up himself, and saw none but the woman, he said unto her, Woman, where are those thine accusers? hath no man condemned thee? 11 She said, No man, Lord. And Jesus said unto her, Neither do I condemn thee: go, and sin no more. John 8:10, 11

Let's Review - The Captive

Our Weapons

For though we walk in the flesh, we do not war after the flesh: 4 (For the weapons of our warfare [are] not carnal, but mighty through God to the pulling down of strong holds;) 5 Casting down imaginations, and every high thing that exalteth itself against the knowledge of God, and bringing into captivity every thought to the obedience of Christ; 6 And having in a readiness to revenge all disobedience, when your obedience is fulfilled. II Corinthians 10:3-6

Whose report will you believe?

The Word of God says that we shall know the truth and the truth will set us free. Where does the Truth come from? Will you believe the Word of God or will you believe your horoscope or someone who reads your palm. Will you believe the creation — or the Creator? Will you cleave to the Divine DNA or Adam's DNA.

Who hath believed our report? and to whom is the arm of the LORD revealed? Isaiah 53:1

We cannot vacillate back and forth, either the battle is

the Lord's or we will fight with our carnal mind – our earthly knowledge, with the Adamic DNA. We cannot be double minded and expect to remain free.

Renounce the bondage

Pray for the blindness to come off the mind of the captive so that He may see Jesus, the Author and Finisher of his faith. The Captive must reach out to God, we can do part of the warfare but the captive must make his own decisions so that he will remain free.

Therefore seeing we have this ministry, as we have received mercy, we faint not; 2 But have renounced the hidden things of dishonesty, not walking in craftiness, nor handling the word of God deceitfully; but by manifestation of the truth commending ourselves to every man's conscience in the sight of God. 3 But if our gospel be hid, it is hid to them that are lost: 4 In whom the god of this world hath blinded the minds of them which believe not, lest the light of the glorious gospel of Christ, who is the image of God, should shine unto them. II Cor. 4:1-4

What does renounce mean?

Renounce means to "**disown.**" Whatever chain the captive has, he must let it go and "disown" it. Repent of it and Walk away from it. One day Jesus showed me a field with a "No Trespassing" sign on it. When we belong to Jesus the devil is a trespasser. Tell him. We must let go of all of the lies, dishonesty, craftiness and sins that open the door for "the Trespasser." Once we belong to God we have the right to tell the "the Trespasser" to get off and never come back.

What did Jesus do?

What did Jesus do when He was confronted with Spiritual Warfare?

After Jesus was in the wilderness and conquered Satan by not giving into temptation, He went into the Temple with a testimony, and with a declaration of His purpose in life.

Read from Luke 4:

1 And Jesus being full of the Holy Ghost returned from Jordan, and was led by the Spirit into the wilderness, 2 Being forty days tempted of the devil. And in those days he did eat nothing: and when they were ended, he afterward hungered. 3 And the devil said unto him, If thou be the Son of God, command this stone that it be made bread. 4 And Jesus answered him, saying, It is written, That man shall not live by bread alone, but by every word of God. 5 And the devil, taking him up into an high mountain, shewed unto him all the kingdoms of the world in a moment of time. 6 And the devil said unto him, All this power will I give thee, and the glory of them: for that is delivered unto me; and to whomsoever I will I give it. 7 If thou therefore wilt worship me, all shall be thine. 8 And Jesus answered and said unto him, Get thee behind me, Satan: for it is written, Thou shalt worship the Lord thy God, and him only shalt thou serve. 9 And he brought him to Jerusalem, and set him on a pinnacle of the temple, and said unto him, If thou be the Son of God, cast thyself down from hence: 10 For it is written, He shall give his angels charge over thee, to keep thee: 11 And in [their] hands they shall bear thee up, lest at any time thou dash thy foot against a stone. 12 And Jesus answering said unto him, It is said, Thou shalt not tempt the Lord thy God. 13 And when the devil had ended all the temptation, he departed from him for a season. 14 And Jesus returned in the power of the Spirit into Galilee: and

there went out a fame of him through all the region round about.

18 The Spirit of the Lord [is] upon me, because he hath anointed me to preach the gospel to the poor; he hath sent me to heal the brokenhearted, to preach deliverance to the captives, and recovering of sight to the blind, to set at liberty them that are bruised, 19 To preach the acceptable year of the Lord.

This is the purpose of Jesus coming to the earth! That He might set us free! It is what God wants for us that we may be brought back to the Father. Oh, if Adam and Eve had not chosen to listen to the Devil! Oh, that we would realize all that God has for us and stop listening to those created beings, but listen to the Creator of the Universe. How free we would be! What a powerful perspective from the One who sees ALL of the past, the present, the future and the eternity... You must make up your mind – Life or Death, Freedom or Bondage, Good or Evil. We cannot have both.

If any of you lack wisdom, let him ask of God, that giveth to all [men] liberally, and upbraideth not; and it shall be given him. 6 But let him ask in faith, nothing wavering. For he that wavereth is like a wave of the sea driven with the wind and tossed. 7 For let not that man think that he shall receive any thing of the Lord. 8 A double minded man [is] unstable in all his ways.

James 1:5-7

Excerpt from "Don't Measure By Yourself" by Rev. Agnes I. Numer

We are talking about our weapons of our warfare – these weapons aren't carnal they are mighty!

One night at 3 o'clock in the morning, somebody knocks on my door and says, "Sister Numer this is an emergency or we wouldn't be here." The man and woman had been coming to our meetings but we didn't know too much about them. He brought her in. I sent my son, David over to the other apartment to sleep somewhere else. We turned that room into a deliverance room. Only I'd never done any deliverance in my life! I walked in and the man was so exhausted from taking his wife to every church in LA. They said, "Go take her to a mental hospital, we can't help her." The wife said, "I was in a church and God brought me to my right mind and He said take her to Sis. Numer and she will help her." I didn't know I would help her. I started praying about it. They brought her. She was out of her mind. I stood there and I looked out of my big window, I could see the mountains, I looked out there and I said, "Jesus what am I going to do?" He said, "You are not going to do anything, I am." He came in that window – right into me.

Jesus did the deliverance of that woman; I had never had anything like it in my life. All night Jesus taught me step by step. He would anoint me. The powers in her would lie to me. It was my training, so that I would know how to do it – when the Lord anointed me – not when I wanted to do it. We prayed for her for a while and then I'd walk in another room, He would let me rest and her rest. After His rest, I would go in to bring deliverance to her.

I learned all about the devil. I learned what they said and how they acted. Their names, they said, "It is Legions." What am I going to do with Legions? I wasn't going to do anything. All night, the rest of the night, Jesus in me delivered that woman. It was 10:30 the next night that the last of them went out of her body and the Spirit of the Lord came and she danced all over the living room – free!

Before she had her deliverance she looked like a witch, she didn't know that the man that she had married was a 69 year old man. She said, "Who is this man?" I said it's your husband. She was only 32 when God set her free. She said, "I don't know Him. I can't go with him." Her folks lived in Arizona. We took that woman and put her on a bus and sent her to Arizona.

This is one of these things that God has done.

And I heard a loud voice saying in heaven, Now is come salvation, and strength, and the kingdom of our God, and the power of his Christ: for the accuser of our brethren is cast down, which accused them before our God day and night. 11 And they overcame him by the blood of the Lamb, and by the word of their testimony; and they loved not their lives unto the death. Revelations 12:10-11

Let's Review - Our Weapons

Spiritual warfare is not a game, it is something that God does through us to help others know Him and become free. This gift from God to us is so that people do not have to spend the rest of their lives tormented and in captivity. Torment was not made for man, hell was not made for man – we must choose to be free to live eternally in His Love, His Peace and His Joy.

We must not agree with the enemy that inner torment is for us and that terrible things must always happen to us. In this world we have tribulation but Jesus has overcome the world! God's eternal life began when we asked Jesus to be our Lord and Savior. That Eternal Kingdom began growing in our hearts. In this Kingdom we have Peace and Joy – no matter the circumstance.

When Jesus was drawn by the Spirit into the wilderness to be tempted of the devil, the greatest weapon Jesus had was that He knew God and that He knew God's Word. He used the Word of God against Satan and Jesus refused to do things against the Nature of God. As we know the Truth, that Truth sets us free.

Take time to know God, to know His Truth, to know His nature – to know Him. When the enemy of God and the enemy of our soul comes – hide in God's presence and obey His command.

The battle is the Lord's.

REVIEW: SPIRITUAL WARFARE

I. The Captain of the Host

WHEN AND HOW DID JESUS:

- Prepare himself for Spiritual Warfare in Luke 4?
- Do Spiritual warfare?
- Cast out devils?

Where does the Bible mention that the Disciples and others – successfully and unsuccessfully cast out devils? Explain what happened.

II. The Warrior

- Define the war.
- What is the battle?
- What is our goal?

III. The Enemy

Critical Thinking Questions

Using the information covered in this session what do you think the answers would be?

If God's enemy had armor what would it look like?
The first one is filled in for you.

Armor Christ

Loins - Truth
Breastplate - Righteousness
Feet - Preparation of The Gospel of Peace
Shield - Faith
Helmet - Salvation
Sword of the Spirit - Word Of God

Armor Anti-Christ

What is the parallel armor of the anti-Christ?

Loins - Deception
Breastplate -
Feet -
Shield -
Helmet -
Sword of the Spirit -

How might God's enemy use the following keys to hold someone captive?

Condemnation
Presumption

IV. The Captive

Critical Thinking Questions
   Using the information covered in this session, how would you answer these questions?

The Captive's Chains

There can be attitudes, addictions, different things that seem to control our lives where we are not free. Name five ways someone may have opened doors to God's enemy and may now be captive:
   a)
   b)
   c)
   d)
   e)

Group Discussion Questions

How do chains get reinforced?
Why are they there?
How will they not come back?
Why did Jesus say go and sin no more?

V. Our Weapons

List five weapons from our Spiritual Warfare Session
a) God's Anointing
b)
c)
d)
e)

Critical Thinking Questions:

When you read the excerpt from "Don't Measure by Yourself" by Rev. Agnes I. Numer, what hope does that give you for spiritual warfare experiences you may encounter or what understanding did it give you from past experiences that you had with spiritual warfare?

QUIZ: SPIRITUAL WARFARE

1. Spiritual warfare is not something we do; it is something God does through us
a. T
b. F

2. Joshua's experience with the Captain of the Hosts teaches us that
a. We might encounter an angel at any time
b. God is not for us – we are for Him
c. The devil can appear as an angel of light

3. God allows difficult circumstances in our lives to strengthen us
a. T
b. F

4. People who "prophesy, cast out devils and do wonderful works" must be doing God's will
a. T

b. F

5. In spiritual warfare we must focus on the enemy
a. T
b. F

6. In spiritual warfare, God's Presence is your key. Select another key below
a. Do not move in presumption
b. Fully focus on what the enemy is doing
c. Keep yourself very busy

7. Focus on what is God doing and saying – right now and:
a. What is this person's greatest need?
b. "God how should we pray in this circumstance?"
c. "What is your direction?"
d. All of the above

8. We should condemn ourselves if an ungodly thought comes to us during warfare
a. T
b. F

9. Spiritual warfare is carried out by the authority of Jesus
a. T
b. F

10. In warfare, when you feel the presence of the spirit of division we should:
a. Pray against it
b. Allow God's love to flow for each other

c. Refuse to give place to it
d. All of the above

11. All of the armor of God is included when we put on Jesus
a. T
b. F

12. After experiencing deliverance, a person might feel empty
a. T
b. F

13. The spiritual weapons we have are mighty through God. They can
a. Pull down of strong holds
b. Cast down imaginations
c. Bring thoughts into captivity to obey Christ
d. All of the above

14. What does renounce mean?
a. To speak critically of someone
b. To disown, repent or walk away
c. An open invitation

15. Jesus conquered Satan by not giving into temptation
a. T
b. F

CHAPTER 5
CONFLICT REVOLUTION

OUR GOALS CAN BE MORE than winning an argument or finding out who is right and who is wrong. Our greatest goal is to believe God that through the conflict there can be a "Revolution"

Revolution definition:

A radical and pervasive change in society and the social structure, especially one made suddenly and often accompanied by violence.

A sudden, extreme, or complete change in the way people live, work, think, etc.

Conflicts are typically not much fun. They can threaten to bring a negative change. They can come up suddenly and unexpectedly. They can lead to breakup of a relationship **OR** they can lead to a radical and powerful change toward deeper relationship; more respect, trust and understanding. **Conflict can be the quickest way to positive changes.** Do not be afraid of conflict. Learn that it is **how we act and respond** which can cause conflicts to bring a much needed "Revolution."

Look at every conflict as an **opportunity:**

- To deepen the relationship.
- To understand one another better, be closer and more open.
- To earn mutual respect.

Guide to positive revolution during a conflict

- **We are on the same side.**

Take the attitude that **this problem is not going to divide us.**

Physically position yourselves so you are both together, facing the problem.

Being seated is a non-threatening position.

Have an attitude of Humility

How have **I** contributed to the problem? **Humility can admit** that I am part of the problem.

Humility can say, "**I'm sorry, forgive me.**"

Pick the Time and Place to talk.

It is not a good time to solve issues when you are too angry. Take time to cool down.

Pick a good place. Not in front of children or other people who do not need to be involved.

- **I value our Relationship.**

Take the time to express your value for the relationship and that you hope to find a solution to the problem at hand.

What is the problem we are trying to solve?

If you can both agree to define the problem you have a chance to solve it.

- **Express your true feelings and listen for what they are really feeling.**

Reflect what they have said by saying, "Let me see if I understand, are you saying that….. or, are you feeling….."

<u>**Seek to truly understand.**</u>

Not listening just to their words but to their heart.

Listen Well.

Often if you will listen well you will get an opportunity to speak and be heard.

Let them know you are listening by your body language and your responses.

Use active listening. "I hear you, I think I understand what you are saying" etc.

Seek Solutions together.

Can we look to God's Word together for an answer? If His word is respected He has an answer.

Here are 10 principles to help us develop deeper relationships:

1. Healing of the Past.

a. When we have been hurt by something in our past which has not yet been healed and someone does something which "feels" similar we can get a flashback of emotions and memories which can cause us to overreact. Our memories can strongly affect our present relationships if we do not forgive and allow God to heal us by His Spirit. God can use current situations to "stir up" old hurts. If we are alert this is a good time to face the past hurts and let Him heal us.

2. God's love, not man's love.

a. Our human love can only go so far. God's love never ends and never gives up. People really need God's love and not our sympathy. We can often be too hard when people need a firm answer and too hard when they really need love and encouragement. Let God love through you. This begins by allowing God's love to penetrate our own hearts. We need a revelation of how much he loves us. Feelings of rejection and abandonment which we have will often be projected onto others when it's not even true.

3. Vows are Forever. They are a promise and a commitment.

a. Go ahead, **pull out your old wedding vows.** Read them over carefully. Let yourself realize that vow is really a commitment… "'till death do us part". There is such a comfort in knowing that we are going to work together to make this work.

b. Divorce is not an option. Never even bring up that word. Don't let it be in your vocabulary or in your mind. Never use it as a threat. Especially when you believe that God joined you together you will not let anyone or anything tear you asunder.

4. Temptations are Parasites.

a. There are vices and habits and addictions which are as destructive as termites and parasites.

   i. When the human body is ravaged by parasites nothing will work right. There is a lot of pain and the body is sick. It is the same in a marriage.

   ii. **Parasites kill.** What begins small can grow and take over the whole relationship and bring its destruction if not treated correctly.

   iii. We have to get rid of habits and addictions which threaten to destroy:

   1. Confess your fault to God.
   2. **Seek an accountability partner.**
   3. Cry out to God for his power to help you overcome.
   4. Do not give up on your first try to overcome. Get up and keep pressing in.

5. Walking in Forgiveness.

a. With God we know that **He is Forgiving.** We can be sure that when we come to Him humbly confessing our sin that He will accept us, He will forgive us and love us.

b. When we walk in love, we walk in forgiveness. We do not decide each time… "will I forgive this time?" Jesus said seventy times seven. When we hold on to things and count how many times… then we are not walking in forgiveness.

c. Revenge must be left to God. When we are angry we are tempted to hurt others with our words and actions. Leave the revenge to God. Do not take it into your own hands.

6. Honor, Respect, Love Cherish.

a. Define these words - Honor, Respect, Love Cherish

b. Men need to be **Respected and Honored.**

i. Learn how to demonstrate respect.

ii. A woman causes all of her children to respect or disrespect her man.

iii. What is important is how you say something more than what you say.

iv. Choose to never speak badly about your mate in public or to your friends. Build them up, honor them and make them special.

a. **Women need to be loved**, cherished and nourished. Look at it like a garden that needs to be watered and tended in order to bring forth fruit.

i. Each woman hears, "I love you" in a different way.

ii. Learn the best ways to say, "I love you" to her.

iii. Make her feel special.

iv. **Speak well of her in private and in public.**

v. Be creative. The fact that you took the time to notice, the trouble to do something, and the care to make it special mean so much.

7. Walk in Humility with each other.

a. Men, learn to say, "I am sorry, I was wrong"

b. Women learn to say, "I forgive you" and accept the apology. Let it go. **Do not bring it up again next argument.**

8. Treat others like they are going to be... Not the way they may be today.

a. See others the way that God sees them. **This takes faith...** see the potential He sees.

b. Don't constantly nag, let God control others and not you.

c. Be patient while He is working. God's not finished with them yet.

9. Respond by the Spirit of the Lord not React by the Flesh.

a. As we learn to walk in the Spirit **we will not fulfill the desires of our flesh.** There are times we would just love to just react and "let them have it" or "blow off steam" and "give them what they deserve". All of these things would be giving into our flesh instead of giving His Spirit the right to control our tongue and our emotions.

b. When we respond by His Spirit then He will deal with them Himself.

c. A soft answer turns away wrath; but grievous answer stirs up wrath.

10. Unconditional Love.

Unconditional synonyms: wholehearted, unqualified, unreserved, unlimited, unrestricted, unmitigated, unquestioning, total, entire, full, absolute, out-and-out, unequivocal.

Unconditional love is what God demonstrates to us. Even while we were still sinners Christ died for us. **The worthy died for the unworthy.** He did not look at our condition as impossible. He reached out in hope that He could touch and change our lives.

a. When we love someone with unconditional love we will find that we cannot do it in our own strength. The ability to love unconditionally only comes from realizing that we have needed unconditional love ourselves. When we realize how much He loves us we can begin to love like He has loved us.

b. **Unconditional love is given freely,** without demanding anything in return. This goes against our fleshly nature.

c. The power of unconditional love is that it is given freely. It is a choice to love.

d. This kind of love is **life changing for both people** involved.

e. It takes faith to love unconditionally and God will see and answer. **God will bring the changes needed.**

Relationships are so rewarding. People add joy and fulfillment to our lives. They can give us so much happiness and pain. Relationships are also hard work. It takes commitment and wisdom. God gives us the Holy Spirit to help us when we need more grace.

Have you ever wondered some time when you prayed

for more patience and grace if He specially sent certain people into your life to develop those virtues you were praying for? We cannot love those people without His help. So we have to call out to Him. When He adds more patience then we can be more patient with everyone around us. Once He has given His gifts to us they are ours. This is how we grow. From Grace to Grace.

2 Peter 1:5-7 And beside this, giving all diligence, add to your faith virtue; and to virtue knowledge; 6 And to knowledge temperance; and to temperance patience; and to patience godliness; 7 And to godliness **brotherly kindness;** and to brotherly kindness, **charity.**

God develops His character in us as we meet people who challenge us. This is a progression from faith, to temperance, to brotherly kindness and finally on to charity... which is God's unconditional love through us. He says we have to **give all diligence** to add His character to ourselves. Please accept the invitation to grow in His character and graces through conflict and difficult people.

Tips for Arguing Fairly

1. Make sure you have enough time to discuss your disagreement.
2. Don't react. Respond by the Spirit of the Lord.
3. Stay to the point. Listen Respectfully.
4. Don't attack the other person's character.
5. Don't bring up the past.
6. Don't argue with an angry person, let them cool down first.
7. Not in front of the children, congregation or others.

8. Always Honor.
9. Always make up later.
10. Choose your battles.
11. Don't go to bed angry.

If we will allow Him, God will help us to turn every Conflict into a Revolution in our own life and in our relationships.

REVIEW: CONFLICT REVOLUTION

Discussion Questions

Describe how God works through relationships to develop His character in us.
Define Conflict Revolution in your own words
Define these four words: Love, Cherish, Respect and Honor
Describe two ways you might show respect to a man that could be meaningful to him?
Describe two ways you might show love to a woman that could be most meaningful to her?
Explain how can hurts of the past affect today? Tell of one experience where this has happened to you.

1. Form 2 groups and practice together (or in pairs) saying, " I am sorry, I was wrong" In this group exercise we will have the men "practice" apologizing and the women will graciously accept that apology. This can be uncomfortable at first. That is why practice is needed. If you are doing

this alone find someone during the day to apologize to. We all offend others so we should be able to find someone.
2. Whose responsibility is it to change other people we are close to?
3. What is our responsibility?

This would be a good time to repent for taking God's job

Review

1. A sudden, extreme change in the way people live, work, think, etc. is called:
a. A conflict
b. A revolution
c. A deal breaker
d. An act of humility

2. An uncomfortable conflict can be the quickest way to positive changes
a. T
b. F

3. Conflicts can lead toward a deeper, more trusting relationship
a. T
b. F

4. A conflict can be an opportunity to:
a. Earn mutual respect

b. Pay the mortgage
c. Make the person pay what they owe you
d. All of the above

5. If you spent too much time listening you will never be able to get your point across
a. T
b. F

6. Select 3 principles that help develop deeper relationships
a. Allow deep sympathy for the person to invade your heart
b. Let God heal you from past issues which arise in present conflicts
c. Learn to love with God's love
d. Realize how habits and addictions are affecting your relationships
e. Nurture your feelings of rejection and abandonment
f. Feel sorry for yourself

7. At a wedding the most important thing is:
a. The wedding cake
b. The color of the dresses
c. The vows you make
d. The kind of pastor who officiates the wedding

8. When we walk in forgiveness we have to decide each time whether to forgive or not.
a. T
b. F

9. Women will flourish fruitfully if you nourish them like a garden that needs to be watered and cared for
a. T
b. F
10. Keep bringing up the past until you have resolved it
a. T
b. F

11. Humility treats people the way they are today
a. T
b. F

12. Choose 4 words which define unconditional love
a. Wholehearted
b. Partiality
c. Unrestricted
d. Unlimited
e. Doubtful
f. Suspicious
g. Unreserved

13. It is never OK to disagree and argue
a. T
b. F

14. Choose 4 points to argue fairly
a. Ramble on and on
b. Listen respectfully
c. Stay to the point. Don't get sidetracked
d. Bring up the past
e. Attack the person

f. Respond, don't react
g. Don't argue when angry
h. Call them bad names

15. When we have said or done something hurtful what should we say?
a. The devil made me do it
b. It is partly your fault
c. I am sorry, I was wrong
d. None of the above

16. Whose responsibility is it to change the person we are close to?
a. His
b. Hers
c. Theirs
d. God's

CHAPTER 6
OF NO REPUTATION

Philippians 2:8-24

8 And being found in fashion as a man, he humbled himself, and became obedient unto death, even the death of the cross.

9 Wherefore God also hath highly exalted him, and given him a name which is above every name:

10 That at the name of Jesus every knee should bow, of things in heaven, and things in earth, and things under the earth;

11 And that every tongue should confess that Jesus Christ is Lord, to the glory of God the Father.

12 Wherefore, my beloved, as ye have always obeyed, not as in my presence only, but now much more in my absence, work out your own salvation with fear and trembling.

13 For it is God which worketh in you both to will and to do of his good pleasure.

14 Do all things without murmurings and disputings:

15 That ye may be blameless and harmless, the sons of

God, without rebuke, in the midst of a crooked and perverse nation, among whom ye shine as lights in the world;

16 Holding forth the word of life; that I may rejoice in the day of Christ, that I have not run in vain, neither laboured in vain.

17 Yea, and if I be offered upon the sacrifice and service of your faith, I joy, and rejoice with you all.

18 For the same cause also do ye joy, and rejoice with me.

19 But I trust in the Lord Jesus to send Timotheus shortly unto you, that I also may be of good comfort, when I know your state.

20 For I have no man likeminded, who will naturally care for your state.

21 For all seek their own, not the things which are Jesus Christ's.

22 But ye know the proof of him, that, as a son with the father, he hath served with me in the gospel.

23 Him therefore I hope to send presently, so soon as I shall see how it will go with me.

24 But I trust in the Lord that I also myself shall come shortly.

I. He Has Forever Taken On The Likeness Of Men

Let's look at the beginning of verse 5. "Let this mind be in you which was also in Christ Jesus: Who, being in the form of God, thought it not robbery to be equal with God: But made Himself of no reputation, and took upon Him the form of a servant, and was made in the likeness of men. And being found in fashion as a man, He humbled Himself, and became obedient unto death, even the death of the cross. Wherefore God hath also highly exalted Him, and given Him a name which is above every name: That at the name of Jesus every knee should bow, of things in heaven, and things in earth, and things under the earth; And that every tongue should confess that Jesus Christ is Lord, to the glory of God the Father."

Why is He saying this to us? In verse 3 He says, "Let nothing be done through strife or vainglory..." 2 But be ye full of joy, likeminded, having the same love, being in one accord and of one mind. "Let this mind be in you which was also in Christ Jesus:"

It's a little bit more difficult for us to be "of no reputation" than it was Jesus. Sometimes we think so, don't we? Jesus is the Son of God and that makes it all the more difficult... because He took the form of man. The likeness of what? "Made in the likeness men."

Maybe it doesn't mean anything to you that Jesus chose the likeness of men. And it doesn't mean a thing to you that He cancelled everything of heaven—everything that was a part of His being in the heavens – He gave it up to be like these little creatures crawling around the earth with two legs, supposedly intelligent, supposedly great people... and still they are. They still think they are above God, and they make God "of no reputation."

One day I was very upset and I said to the Lord, "God, why don't You show this old world who You are? Why?" Then He gave me the Psalm 78 where He said, "And He delivered His strength into captivity, and His glory into the enemy's hand." Psalm 78:61 God has not yet taken all His glory out of the enemy's hand. He hasn't yet released His strength on this earth. **But He's going to do it.** He's shaking Himself right now. The things which are being said and done against Him today ... He's getting ready to shake Himself as one that has been in a deep sleep and He's going to hit His enemies in the "hinder parts." And when He does, something's going to happen. He's going to take His strength out of captivity and His glory away from Satan.

He took on the likeness of men, made Himself "of no reputation," and, being found in fashion as a man, He humbled Himself. You know, no good person could have redeemed mankind. No Son of God could redeem mankind. Only Jesus as the Son of man could redeem man. Whatever He was before He came to this earth, He was never again… because He forever took the form of man, made in the likeness of man. "…and being fashioned as a man, He humbled Himself, and became obedient unto death, even the death of the cross." He made Himself of no reputation, by taking on the form of man – not the Son of God, but the Son of man. He would never, never have the same relationship with the Father when He left heaven to come to earth: He was forever to be fashioned after man.

II. How Can We Not Yield To The Cry Of This Jesus?

How can we? **HOW CAN WE NOT YIELD TO HIS CROSS?** How can we not yield to the cry of the Lord, who humbled Himself? Maybe you don't know what it would mean. I'm sure I don't know what it would mean for the Lord of lords and the King of kings to come and be spit upon, cursed, reviled, persecuted – all the nasty, evil things

– and then end up at the cross: **obedient even unto death for you and I.**

I think we have some nerve to think that we can talk any way to God except to obey Him. I don't know how we think we can go in the way of the world, and compromise in the world, when Jesus made no compromise. How can we do it? We can't do it. Even though we think we can get by with it, we can't get by with it. Because He became "of no reputation" to be like men. It should put us to shame to even think of any way other than God's way.

I remember the day when I sat in a home in India. A young man asked me a question: "Any religion is all right, isn't it? If you believe in it?" Suddenly, something happened to me. The Lord lifted me up into the realm of eternity: it was before time, before man was created. As I was in the realm of eternity, I heard a conversation between God the Father and by His Son, Jesus. I felt the great love of God that has for this one that consented to be of no reputation, but consented to be like men – that He might take us out of the judgment that had already been pronounced on the human race, to take us from the hand of Satan and redeem us back to the Father.

I felt the Father's love for His precious Son and the price that He would pay, as together they began to talk of what He would do for this mankind that they were going to create, knowing full well that man was going to fall in the hands of Satan and be condemned forever without God. Knowing all of this, God created man for His own pleasure.

How can we hesitate tonight and add the world to our pleasure? How can we mix ourselves with the things of the world and think we are doing God's pleasure? How can we do it? How can we even think about these things? "Oh, you have to have this; you have to have that..."

I don't know what I said to the people at that table that day, but one thing I knew: I had been in the presence of Almighty God, and I had been in the presence of His Son, and I knew how God's heart was, and I knew what Jesus' heart was, and I knew the price they decided to pay to have people called human beings on an earth that God created for them, even the price of the cross – even the price of laying His life down to become like man. He didn't have to. God didn't have to have us, but He desired a people that would love Him and serve Him not because He clubbed them to do it, not because He put circumstances that nobody could get around, but because His Son loved us. God so loved us that He sent His Son into the world to die for us. And Jesus so loved us that He gave His life at the cross for us.

Then how can we be so cheap? So cheap that we think we could discredit Him? How can we do it?

And all He's asking of us is to take this life and let it be wholly consecrated unto Him. All He asks is to empty ourselves of the things Satan has put upon us, and let us be filled with His joy, with His love, with His peace, with His righteousness. How can we balance it? How can we justify ourselves in what we say and what we do? How can we do it? We cannot do it... we cannot do it.

III. What If Jesus Had Compromised?

Compromise is a terrible thing in the sight of God. If Jesus had compromised with Satan in the wilderness, there would be no redemption of man. Everyone of us would be doomed to go to hell. We would have gone there without any reprieve from the Lord, had He compromised in the wilderness when Satan was trying to get Him to acknowledge He was the Son of God. He did not come to this earth as the Son of God. He took on the form of man to redeem man by His own stand as the Son of man. He chose to become one of us. He chose to be "of no reputation," that He might bring us into the presence of God, that He might take from our life everything that is against God; that He might be everything unto us. How can we go halfway with God? How can we think we can get by? **No way. NO WAY. The price that He paid was too much.**

I don't know how long I was in the realm of eternity. Time was not there. There was only eternity. But something happened to me there. It was as though the Lord took me to the beginning of time when He created the world, and He put man upon the earth. I watched all of this happening, and I watched it come down to the time that Jesus became like man – in the likeness of man. How they tried to kill Him as soon as He was born. The Pharisees and the Sadducees tried to kill Him; Satan tried to kill Him in the wilderness. But He went in there with power, and He came out with power! Amen! The power of the Holy Ghost!

He won our redemption at the cross, but He won the battle against Satan for us in the wilderness. He fought this battle as the Son of man, He did not fight it as the Son of God. Satan tried to tempt Jesus to respond as the Son of God, but He would not respond as the Son of God. He knew He had come as the Son of man, and He must go to the cross as the Son of man, not as the Son of God. He laid it down for you and I. **He laid His it down for the whole world.** Down through the generations of time.

Again I was observing what was taking place: all that happened to Jesus and at the cross, and after His death, and after His resurrection. Then after His resurrection, the scene changed. Something happened at the resurrection. Jesus completed what the Father sent Him to do. It was to bring all mankind that would come to him back to the Father, back to God, with their sins forgiven, their lives transformed.

When He arose from the dead, the Bible says the saints arose with Him. Doesn't it? Do you know what happened to those saints? **They're up there waiting for you and I to get saintly!** They're up there waiting. A host that no man can number looking down here saying, "Why don't you people let God do what He needs to do with you? You're slowing down the time of the coming of the Lord." They're not pitying you. They're disturbed because you're taking too much time! You're not letting God do the work He needs to do, so Jesus can come again. This same Jesus died on the cross and rose again. This same Jesus forgives us of our sins. This same Jesus is coming again. And this is what He says: "Wherefore God also has highly exalted Him, and given Him a name, which is above every name: That at the name of Jesus every knee should bow, of things in heaven, and things in earth, and things under the earth; And that every tongue should confess that Jesus Christ is Lord, to the glory of God the Father." Amen.

IV. Every Knee Is Going To Bow

What is it to us, to pay this price that we may be able to stand before Him that **He may make us as He is?** Then why do we compromise? Why do we allow the things of this world, and the devil, and people, and things to hinder us from entering into that place in Him where we can know that it is Christ in us? We can know that this love changes our lives.

The same mind that Jesus had, He's giving to us – that we might do the will of the Father, through Jesus Christ, who died for us. He rose again, and it doesn't matter whether they believe it or don't believe it. It doesn't matter if they are wicked or not wicked. It doesn't matter where they stand before God tonight. It doesn't matter. "Every knee is going to bow, and every tongue is going to confess that Jesus Christ is Lord." They're going to do it, and they might do it in their anger or in their hate, or in their total destruction of their soul, but they're going to do it.

Whether they like it or not.

The day's coming and they're going to have to declare it. I don't think it's far off, because our Lord paid a price for us to be filled with the fullness of God – the very fullness of God. Jesus paid the price that we might stand before Him in the Day of Judgment – boldly stand before Him. Not of our boldness, but in the honest humility of Jesus Christ. Stand there humble, in the very presence of the Son of God, that we might be as He is.

V. What Will It Mean To Jesus?

Can you think about what it would mean to Jesus, when He sees that multitude that has become just like He is? He's going to present the kingdom to the Father. This kingdom that Satan took away from God, he thinks he's winning over it all. No, he isn't, because one day our Lord Jesus is going to say, "Come with Me. I want you to go with Me while I present the kingdom of this world." **The kingdom that Jesus brought to this world.** Not the worldly kingdom. "Come on, it's time now to present it to the Father." What do you think the Father's going to do when He looks at us and sees Jesus? He doesn't see us, He sees Jesus. That's what He looks at now, and He sees Jesus shaping and molding our lives so that He can say, "Come on, family, I want to present you to My Father." Jesus became the Son of man with no reputation, that we might become sons of God – that we might join with Him.

How do we have the nerve? How do we think we have the nerve to do this to Jesus? How do we have the nerve to let our lives be compromising and half full of the devil and half full of ourselves, instead of giving it all to Jesus, and allowing Jesus to come forth in us? I think we need to consider it and see where we stand in Him, because He wants us to stand in all the fullness of the Father.

To do that, every tongue must confess that Jesus Christ is Lord, to the glory of God the Father. I hope that today this message stirs your heart such as you've never been stirred in all your life, and it will make you turn around and become "of no reputation," like Jesus. That you would realize that Jesus did it for us, that we might be able to bow before Him, and give Him the glory. Give Him the glory for every little thing that He gives to us. Every ray of hope, everything that we have, the Lord has given to us. Let's shake ourselves from all these other things.

VI. All He Asks Is For Us To Give Him Our All

I knew a young man who walked away from what God had for him. How can someone walk away, when God has done so much in his life? We might play games with people, but we don't play games with God. **Jesus paid it all... to give us all that the Father has for us.** It's ours today and all He asks is for us to give Him our all and He will take it and He will give to us His all. He already paid the price for us, so that one day we can stand before Him boldly and know that He has made us as He is, through His precious blood, and in His mighty name. He has transformed our lives.

God is saying, "Surrender all to Jesus."

You're going to meet this message down the road somewhere. You heard it and God will hold you responsible. You'll meet it down the road. I encourage you to meet it before judgment comes. I hope you decided today to let Jesus be all in all to you. I hope you lay everything down at Jesus' feet, and let Him become to you the Lord of lords and the King of kings. Praise His name.

"...it is God which worketh in you both to will and to do of His good pleasure...That ye may be blameless and harmless, the sons of God, without rebuke, in the midst of a crooked and perverse nation, among whom ye shine as lights in the world; Holding forth the word of life; that I may rejoice in the day of Christ, that I have not run in vain, neither laboured in vain." Philippians 2:13, 15, 16

Closing Prayer

Father, we thank You. Jesus, we thank You that You became "of no reputation" like unto man. And, Lord, we wonder how you could die for such as these. O God, only You must say we are "of no reputation" except in Jesus. Lord, this night, bring forth Your Spirit in us. Let true repentance come to every one of our hearts, that this light which is in us shall become brighter; that we may walk without compromise in this world today; that the light shall become brighter and brighter unto the perfect day. We give You glory. We thank You for this Word. We ask You, our God, bring us to the realization that there is no compromise in God. It's all in all or none at all. Today, Lord Jesus, speak to our hearts about everything we're trying to compromise with. We ask You, Jesus, to take us, and let us see ourselves as You see us, that we might stand before You, set free in the light of Christ to be revealed in us. We thank You, Lord, for this Word. We thank You for the ears that have heard it and the hearts that have received it, and, Lord, we give You glory for it now, that You will bring it to pass. In Your Wonderful Name we ask it, and for Your glory. Amen.

REVIEW: OF NO REPUTATION

True or False

1. ___ Jesus gave up only a part of what He was in the heavens to become like man.
2. ___ Jesus hasn't yet taken all His glory out of the enemy's hand.
3. ___ Only the Son of God could have redeemed man.
4. ___ Now Jesus has the same relationship with the Father as He did before He came to earth.
5. ___ We can go in the way of the world.
6. ___ It should put us to shame to think of any other way than God's way.
7. ___ God created man for His own pleasure even though He knew man would fall into the hands of Satan.
8. ___ God desires a people that would love Him and serve Him, not because He clubbed them to do it, not because He put circumstances that nobody could get around, but because His Son loved us.
9. ___ Jesus won the battle for us at the cross.

10. ___ Jesus completed what the Father sent Him to do at the resurrection.

11. ___ The saints are waiting for you and I to allow God to do what He needs to do with us.

12. ___ We could never have the same mind Jesus had.

13. ___ Every knee is going to bow and every tongue is going to confess that Jesus Christ is Lord.

14. ___ When we stand before Him in the day of judgment, it will be in the honest humility of Jesus Christ.

15. ___ Jesus is going to present to the father a multitude of people that have become just like He is.

16. ___ He became the Son of man with no reputation, that we might become sons of God.

17. ___ We might play games with people, but we don't play games with God.

18. ___ Every ray of hope, everything that we have, the Lord has given to us.

19. ___ All he's asking of us is to take this life and let it be wholly consecrated unto Him.

20. ___ This message should stir our hearts, and make us turn around to become "of no reputation" like Jesus.

CHAPTER 7
SHEPHERDS AND SHEEP

Let's go straight to the Bible to see what we can learn how God expects Pastors and Leaders or Shepherds to behave toward His flock.

Let's read Ezekiel 34.

Ezekiel 34: Then the word of the Lord came to me saying, 2 "Son of man, prophesy against the shepherds of Israel. Prophesy and say to those shepherds, 'Thus says the Lord God, "Woe, shepherds of Israel who have been feeding themselves! Should not the shepherds feed the flock? 3 You eat the fat and clothe yourselves with the wool, you slaughter the fat sheep without feeding the flock. 4 Those who are sickly you have not strengthened, the diseased you have not healed, the broken you have not bound up, the scattered you have not brought back, nor have you sought for the lost; but with force and with severity you have dominated them.

Read the following verses and fill in the blanks in this chart

What those Shepherd were doing	What True Shepherds would do

When people in our care fall into false beliefs, wander away, become offended or simply stop attending our services, we can easily blame them or become disgusted at their behavior. This is not what God desires in a Good Shepherd.

Read verse 5 and describe what a good Shepherd does when a sheep in their care becomes "lost".

5 They were scattered for lack of a shepherd, and they became food for every beast of the field and were scattered. 6 My flock wandered through all the mountains and on every high hill; My flock was scattered over all the surface of the earth, and there was no one to search or seek for them.

What does God say in the following verses that he is going to do about the irresponsible and selfish shepherds?

_____

_____

7 THEREFORE, YOU SHEPHERDS, HEAR THE WORD OF THE LORD: 8 "As I live," declares the Lord God, "surely because

My flock has become a prey, My flock has even become food for all the beasts of the field for lack of a shepherd, and My shepherds did not search for My flock, but rather the shepherds fed themselves and did not feed My flock; 9 therefore, you shepherds, hear the word of the Lord: 10 'Thus says the Lord God, "Behold, I am against the shepherds, and I will demand My sheep from them and make them cease from feeding sheep. So the shepherds will not feed themselves anymore, but I will deliver My flock from their mouth, so that they will not be food for them.

Notice also that there is a subtle change in wording. Instead of God talking about "the flock" he begins to say, "MY flock".

11 For thus says the Lord God, "Behold, I Myself will search for My sheep and seek them out. 12 As a shepherd cares for his herd in the day when he is among his scattered sheep, so I will care for My sheep and will deliver them from all the places to which they were scattered on a cloudy and gloomy day.

This is what God, who is the Good Shepherd, promises He will do for his flock.

13 I will bring them out from the peoples and gather them from the countries and bring them to their own land; and I will feed them on the mountains of Israel, by the streams, and in all the inhabited places of the land. 14 I will feed them in a good pasture, and their grazing ground will be on the mountain heights of Israel. There they will lie down on good grazing ground and feed in rich pasture on

the mountains of Israel. 15 I will feed My flock and I will lead them to rest," declares the Lord God. 16 "I will seek the lost, bring back the scattered, bind up the broken and strengthen the sick;

In the next verses there is more to the promise which was partially pointing to King David but ultimately to Jesus who came out of the lineage of David.

23 "Then I will set over them one shepherd, My servant David, and he will feed them; he will feed them himself and be their shepherd. 24 And I, the Lord, will be their God, and My servant David will be prince among them; I the Lord have spoken.

In John 10 Jesus said about himself, "**I am The Good Shepherd**... (Who) gives his life for the sheep". He was probably referring to Ezekiel 34, since there are many things that sound similar. When Jesus said this the religious leaders who were listening became so angry they picked up stones to kill Jesus. Perhaps they knew the passage in Ezekiel and understood that Jesus was referring to them as being the uncaring shepherds. God was getting ready to fulfill this promise through His Son.

7 So Jesus said to them again, "Truly, truly, I say to you, I am the door of the sheep. 8 All who came before Me are thieves and robbers, but the sheep did not hear them. 9 I am the door; if anyone enters through Me, he will be saved, and will go in and out and find pasture. 10 The thief comes only to steal and kill and destroy; I came that they may have life, and have it abundantly. 11 "I am the good shepherd; the good shepherd lays down His life for the sheep. 12 He who is a hired hand, and not a shepherd, who is not the owner of the sheep, sees the wolf coming, and leaves the sheep and

flees, and the wolf snatches them and scatters them. 13 He flees because he is a hired hand and is not concerned about the sheep. 14 I am the good shepherd, and I know My own and My own know Me, 15 even as the Father knows Me and I know the Father; and I lay down My life for the sheep."

Jesus makes it clear that He is **not only talking about the children of Israel** when He says, "My flock". He came to lay down His life for people around the world to be able to come into "the sheep fold".

John 10:16 I have other sheep, which are not of this fold; I must bring them also, and they will hear My voice; and they will become one flock with one shepherd. 17 For this reason the Father loves Me, because I lay down My life so that I may take it again. 18 No one has taken it away from Me, but I lay it down on My own initiative. I have authority to lay it down, and I have authority to take it up again. This commandment I received from My Father."

Jesus called each of his disciples with the same call, "Follow Me" Then He added, **"And I will make you fishers of men."** After Jesus' death, when all of the disciples had fled and Peter had denied him 3 times, Jesus found Peter. He was fishing, not for men, but for fish - and they caught nothing. Jesus appeared to them and He challenged Peter.

Read John 21:15–17. Describe what Jesus challenged and called Peter to do:

_____

_____

Would this mean that Peter was called to be a Shepherd? Was Jesus calling forth a new order of Shepherds?

Think about these questions while reading 1 Peter 5:1-4. Remember that Peter himself is writing this letter.

> *1 Peter 5:1 Therefore, I exhort the elders among you, as your fellow elder and witness of the sufferings of Christ, and a partaker also of the glory that is to be revealed, 2 shepherd the flock of God among you, exercising oversight not under compulsion, but voluntarily, according to the will of God; and not for sordid gain, but with eagerness; 3 nor yet as lording it over those allotted to your charge, but proving to be examples to the flock. 4 And when the Chief Shepherd appears, you will receive the unfading crown of glory.*

Peter is calling the elders among them, "fellow elders". He did not raise himself above them but instead lifted up Christ as the Chief Shepherd and all of them including himself as "Under Shepherds". These "New order" of Shepherds are under the direction of Christ. It is **His Flock** that we care for. Jesus was taking the care of His people out of the hands of irresponsible shepherds - the Pharisees and the law, and placing them under the care of men empowered and lead by the Holy Spirit.

Let's Read Acts 20:28

"*Take heed therefore unto yourselves, and to all the flock, over the which the Holy Ghost hath made you overseers, to feed the church of God, which he hath purchased with his own blood.*"

Paul called the elders (*PRESBUETROS*) of the church and **challenged them to be overseers** (*EPISKOPOS*) (Acts 20:17)

- They must "Be on guard" for the flock

- The **Holy Spirit was the one who had made them overseers** not Paul. Paul's letters let us know that Timothy, Titus and Paul all chose leaders in every church they established and set them as leaders
- They were to Shepherd the church which belongs to Jesus who paid for it with His own blood.
- Verse 31 They were to "Be on the alert" because of the "grievous wolves"
- Verse 35 Paul reminded them that Jesus had taught them, "It is more blessed to give than to receive". Paul cites his own life as an example how he provided for his own needs by the work of his own hands. He did not take anything from them.

Our leadership, to be Christ like, cannot be like the shepherds in Ezekiel 34, who "with force and with severity … dominated them". It must be with love. Jesus asked Peter, "do you love me?" He asked him three times just like Peter had denied Him three times. Jesus said that a good shepherd, "lays his life down for the sheep". This kind of **love only comes from the Holy Spirit** through us. He can empower us to love His Flock with His love and to tend them, guard them, feed them, shepherd them, protect them, and lead them.

David's Shepherd Psalm 23 expresses his heart toward the Lord, his good Shepherd. Through all of the crises and victories of his life the Lord had been a very Good Shepherd to him. Recognizing God's love for him in every situation also made David a good shepherd to his people when he became the nation's leader. If we allow God to love us and Shepherd us we also will learn to be loving shepherds.

Let's Read Psalm 23:

> *23 The Lord is my shepherd; I shall not want. 2 He maketh me to lie down in green pastures: he leadeth me beside the still waters. 3 He restoreth my soul: he leadeth me in the paths of righteousness for his name's sake. 4 Yea, though I walk through the valley of the shadow of death, I will fear no evil: for thou art with me; thy rod and thy staff they comfort me. 5 Thou preparest a table before me in the presence of mine enemies: thou anointest my head with oil; my cup runneth over. 6 Surely goodness and mercy shall follow me all the days of my life: and I will dwell in the house of the Lord for ever.*

David wrote this "Shepherd Psalm" to show us what a Good Shepherd is really like. Pray now that God will fill you with His Spirit and make you a **good Shepherd** of His flock because one day we will all stand before Him for the things we have said and done and for how we have cared for the least of these our brethren.

REVIEW: SHEPHERDS AND SHEEP

Discussion Questions

In your own words, explain the following phrases in 1 Peter 5, which help us understand what is a good Shepherd:

1. not under compulsion, but voluntarily
2. according to the will of God
3. not for sordid gain
4. with eagerness
5. not lording it over (them)
6. be examples to the flock
7. receive the "unfading crown of glory"

Review Questions

1. In Ezekiel 34 God speaks out through the prophet about the shepherds who were not serving God's sheep very well. **Choose 6** ways you find in this chapter that they were not doing well.

a. They were feeding themselves instead of the sheep
b. Getting Fat off the sheep
c. Clothing themselves with the wool
d. Gathering the sheep
e. Not caring for the sick
f. Protecting the sheep
g. Not drawing back the scattered
h. Patiently training their flock
i. Seeking God's will for the sheep
j. Leading by their examples
k. Dominating them with force and severity
l. Ministering healing to the afflicted

2. In John 10:16 Jesus explains that the sheep are the children of Israel only
a. T
b. F

3. When Jesus met Peter on the shore after he had denied him, he asked him one question 3 times
a. Peter, "Do you love me?"
b. Will you fish for men?
c. Will you lead my church?
d. Will you sell all you have and follow me?

4. What did Jesus tell Peter to do, 3 times following each question?
a. Gather the disciples daily
b. Fish in the daytime
c. Feed my sheep

5. With Peter a new order of shepherding was being established which was Christ like and would love the sheep with His love.
a. True
b. False

6. Looking at 1 Peter 5:1-4. **Choose 6** ways Peter exhorted the leaders lead their "flocks"
a. Not under compulsion but voluntarily
b. Dominating them with force
c. Getting Fat off the sheep
d. According to the will of God
e. Not for sordid gain
f. Scatter your sheep
g. Make them do what even you would not do
h. With eagerness
i. Not lording it over them
j. Be examples to the flock
k. Treat them severely
l. Receive the unfading crown of glory

7. What promise do we find in 1 Peter 5:4 for faithful shepherds who follow these exhortations?
a. Have the largest churches in your cities
b. Exponential church growth
c. You will receive the crown of glory when he appears
d. Your finances will grow miraculously

CHAPTER 8
FAITH WORKETH BY LOVE

Opening Prayer

FATHER, we praise You. We, thank You, for Your hallowed presence. We, thank You, for honoring us with Your presence. We, thank You, for honoring us Lord, to be Your servants to obey You. Today, Jesus, speak to our hearts. Make plain the Word before us that we might write it on our heart, that we might not sin against You. For the Living Word, thank You Jesus. Bless this people Jesus with Your richest blessings. Oh, God,

You know every need and You're the One that can meet those needs. We thank You Lord Jesus. Father, we thank You for the Word of God. We thank You now for what You're doing in each of our lives. Preparing us to be sent by You wherever You choose for us to go. We, thank You, Jesus. Lord, let this Word be what You want it to be to each of us and we magnify Your name and give You glory in Jesus name. Amen.

I. For We Through The Spirit Wait For the Hope of Righteousness by Faith

Let's turn to Galatians chapter 5. I think this chapter is very important to each of our lives. The Lord spoke to me in the wee hours of the morning concerning it.

> 1. Stand fast therefore in the liberty wherewith Christ hath made us free, and be not entangled again with the yoke of bondage.
> 2. Behold, I Paul say unto you, that if ye be circumcised, Christ shall profit you nothing.
> 3. For I testify again to every man that is circumcised, that he is a debtor to do the whole law.
> 4. Christ is become of no effect unto you, whosoever of you are justified by the law; ye are fallen from grace.
> 5. For we through the Spirit wait for the hope of righteousness by faith.
> 6. For in Jesus Christ neither circumcision availeth any thing, nor uncircumcision; but faith which worketh by love.
> 7. Ye did run well; who did hinder you that ye should not obey the truth?
> 8. This persuasion cometh not of him that calleth you.
> 9. A little leaven leaveneth the whole lump.
> 10. I have confidence in you through the Lord, that ye will be none otherwise minded: but he that troubleth you shall bear his judgment, whosoever he be.
> 11. And I, brethren, if I yet preach circumcision, why do I yet suffer persecution? Then is the offense of the cross ceased.

12. I would they were even cut off which trouble you.

13. For, brethren, ye have been called unto liberty; only use not liberty for an occasion to the flesh, but by love serve one another.

14. For all the law is fulfilled in one word, even in this; Thou shall love thy neighbor as thyself.

15. But if ye bite and devour one another, take heed that ye be not consumed one of another.

16. This I say then, Walk in the Spirit, and ye shall not fulfill the lust of the flesh.

17. For the flesh lusteth against the Spirit, and the Spirit against the flesh: and these are contrary the one to the other: so that ye cannot do the things that ye would.

18. But if ye be led of the Spirit, ye are not under the law.

19. Now the works of the flesh are manifest, which are these; adultery, fornication, uncleanness, lasciviousness,

20. Idolatry, witchcraft, hatred, variance, amulations, wrath, strife, seditions, heresies,

21. Envyings, murders, drunkenness, revellings, and such like: of the which I tell you before, as I have also told you in time past, that they which do so such things shall not inherit the kingdom of God.

22. But the fruit of the Spirit is love, joy, peace, longsuffering, gentleness, goodness, faith,

23. Meekness, temperance: against such there is no law.

24. And they that are Christ's have crucified the flesh with the affections and lusts.

25. If we live in the Spirit, let us also walk in the Spirit.

26. Let us not be desirous of vain glory, provoking one another, envying one another.

Isn't that a powerful word?

"For we through the Spirit wait for the hope of righteousness by faith." (Gal. 5:5)

We are made righteous in Christ with His righteousness. There's one little word here. Did you catch it? **Love.**

Sometimes by the way we act toward one another we wouldn't know that we love one another. I praise the Lord for the love of God. God is changing our lives because we have His love, we also have a lot of things still in our lives that war against His love. Isn't this true? So what has to happen here? Something has to change. His love isn't going to change so we have to change. We have to allow Him to change us. Now, I know as a human being we're very sensitive. If we're in the flesh we're even more sensitive, and we're looking for trouble, we find it. You find it even among those who love you because we're not quite out of the woods ourselves.

What Paul is saying is very plain. In the first place there is only one way that our love is going to operate and His faith operate in us. He's talking about "without works", our faith is no good to us. Now, there are a lot of "works" in the world today and they're by "faith" but not really by faith. They call it faith but they organize everything and there's no room for God to organize anything. They call their works "by faith." But God has a way by His Spirit that He wants to lead us, not under the law, but by grace.

Now I think that grace is tolerant, isn't it? It's not like the law. Sometimes we get like the law don't we and we don't bend in any direction? We kind of get "this is the way it is", you know? But grace comes along and says "Let's have some mercy on it." Then we learn not everybody is at the same spiritual level as we are.

So God is good. He doesn't measure us by ourselves or one another. He measures us by His light. We're walking in His light, not in our lights, you're not walking in my light, I'm not walking in your light, I'm walking in the light of the Lord. He's giving it to you and then you have to walk in it. There are certain things that we need to do as we're walking with Jesus. He said if we live in the spirit, then we must walk in the Spirit and sometimes our flesh gets in the way. We get confused. The Lord is very clear here, what is of the Spirit and what is not of the Spirit. If we get over in this little territory that isn't of His Spirit, we need to recognize it immediately and do something about it.

He said if we're led by the Spirit we're under grace, we're not under the law. We have to remember we're not under the law. Maybe our brother and sister doesn't see things exactly the way we see it but remember, they're not walking in your light, they're walking in His light that He has given to them. Now remember when we come to Jesus He changes our life. He brings us to His kingdom. In Him is life and when we allow Him to come into our life, and we are forgiven of our sins then something happens inside of us.

We're in a new kingdom. We're not under the law but we're under grace and grace abounds for us. **We have to be careful that we're not trying to pull somebody else the way we want them to go but we direct them to Christ.** For it's Christ in us that's the hope of glory. Not how somebody thinks about it, not how we think about it, but it's Jesus in us.

He's the one that brings His Spirit and causes us to walk in His Spirit. When we walk in His Spirit the word says we don't fulfill the things of the flesh. We need to realize that He's saying two things. He's saying the works of the flesh are one thing but the fruit of the Spirit is love. **God is saying to us, walk away, as far as you can go from the works of the flesh;** go straight to the cross and you go to Jesus. In your heart you have to have a determination that you're going to separate yourself from that flesh. You're not going to allow the flesh to rule but you're going before the cross, you're going to give it to Jesus and you're determined you want to be free. Now He said, "don't use that freedom for an occasion of the flesh" and sometimes we do, but God will speak to us about it.

II. The Law Of The Spirit Of Life In Christ Jesus

He said if we're led by the Spirit we're under a new law. That law which we have by the Spirit of God under grace is the law of the Spirit of life in Christ Jesus. It has made us free from the law of sin and death. Many Christians are still living under the law of sin and death. They do not realize that there's a new law that's operating inside of them and they need to allow Jesus to take care of the things that need to be done. We have a new law in us and that law is the law of the Spirit of Life in Christ Jesus. Now with this law there's a fruit that comes from this new relationship that we have with Jesus. The fruit of the law of life is God's love, God's joy, His peace, His longsuffering, gentleness, goodness, faith, meekness, temperance, against such there is no law.

Remember that, there is no law against it. There are laws against the works of the flesh. If we get out there doing the works of the flesh we're liable to end up in prison but not with the law of the Spirit of Life. We're free from the law of sin and death. We're not under that law. We're not out there sinning like the world does but we have to remember that there's a way we have to walk. We have to walk in the spirit.

There are things that the Lord has to do. A lot of deliverance must come to us, isn't that right? We have to be set free from the old law of sin and death. Now when we're water baptized, the Bible says the old man is buried. Isn't that exciting?

I was raised a Nazarene and you had to fight the old man all the days of your life. But one day the Lord showed me it wasn't true. It was very mighty how He showed it to me. I was ministering on water baptism and all of a sudden the Lord took me into a realm that I knew nothing about. The meeting lasted two whole hours. He took me in to the watery grave with Him and He showed me what it meant to be baptized in water into His death.

We carry the old man right there, we bury him and he's no longer a part of us. Then we realize we come up a new creature, a new creation with a new life in us and the old things pass away. The law is fulfilled but grace comes there with us. As the Lord gave me this experience He took me down; He took the keys away from Satan and handed them to me. It was an awesome time. The glory and presence of the Lord filled the living room as He began to reveal His word as it was, as it is to us today.

We don't have to struggle with the old man of sin, we have to get rid of him by water baptism. Give him to Jesus and He buries it down there. You see, we can't get forgiveness for it because we didn't commit it. We can take the old man of sin and bury him. The responsibility is then ours, we can't blame it on the old man of sin.

After water baptism if there are things in our life, we have to remember we're responsible to get them out and get rid of them. The old man... that sinful nature is dead and buried so we can't blame him any more. Christians blame the old sinful nature if they do something wrong but it doesn't work because the word says that sinful nature is dead and buried through water baptism and now you are accountable and you will have to stand before God.

III. If We Walk In the Spirit Then We're Walking In His Love

God said here I have a new walk for you, it's a walk in the Spirit. If you live in the Spirit then you walk in the Spirit. What happens to a lot of people? They don't realize what Jesus has done for them. They go around carrying all these and think they have to because the old man is there and there's nothing we can do about it. But this is not true, he's not there. So we're responsible to get rid of it ourselves. If we get some hangovers of the old life then we better cut them off and say "Lord, I don't want them... I want to walk in the Spirit, I want to live in the Spirit, I want the Spirit of the Lord to have His way in me."

If we walk in the Spirit then we're walking in His love because the fruit of His Spirit is love. You know when you come to Jesus how full of love you feel? So mighty is that love when you turn your life over to Him and then His joy, and His peace comes you. You have new life. You're a new creature in Christ Jesus.

Then let's see how fast we can get rid of the works of the flesh. People make mistakes and maybe they don't talk to you the way they ought to but they have to answer to God for it, not you. But, the way you take it? You will have to answer to God for it. We have to be careful that we're not affected by people. We are all human beings and we are all learning how to walk in the Spirit. We don't want to be contaminated with the works of man, we want to be free in the love of God and know that Jesus provided that love for you by His Spirit so that His pure love can flow and you can be free. **God's love is the answer.**

Sometimes we get busy, we forget that the natural and the spiritual have to flow together or we have a collision, don't we? What's the matter today in a world of Christianity? We got so spiritual that we forgot the natural. God said we have to bring the spiritual into the natural so that the natural becomes spiritual and the spiritual becomes natural. Only then, can we flow together without bumping against one another. We flow together because we're in the Spirit of God. The most important training is to teach us to flow by the Spirit of God.

The Lord spoke this to me, "if you just tell them to pray for this food and the people that are receiving it then God is going to work with them. They're going to know. You won't want to take a nap in between because God's strength and joy will be with you. As you're praying for them God's love is going out to them.

Did you know that if a person doesn't have anybody to pray for them God can't save them? You know why? Because God has to be asked to save them. There has to be someone who cares enough to pray for them because God will not just go out and force anybody to come to Him. Someone has to care enough to be the intercessor that will draw them to God.

IV. God Is Calling Us To Be Trained By His Spirit

We're living in an awesome time. We're living in a time when the gathering of the nations are coming before God. We have to be faithful in bringing this gospel of the kingdom of Jesus Christ to the nations of the world. There's a world out there in Denominationalism, Moslem, Hinduism, Buddhism, Atheism and they don't know Jesus. This is the day the Lord is pouring out His Spirit. This is the day that He's training us to flow by His Spirit, filling us with His love because that love is what is going to change the lives of people.

God is calling us to be trained by His Spirit so that when we go out there God's love is going to draw them. **God's peace, His joy, His righteousness is there to draw them unto Him. The world is looking for God's love.** This morning I feel that love so much. The Lord is saying let us live in the Spirit and let us walk in the spirit. Show forth His love, His peace, His joy, longsuffering, gentleness, goodness and faith, meekness, temperance. This I like very much; they can't arrest you for that. There's no law against it. They can't take it from you... so walk in it.

It's so mighty what God is doing. We must all be trained by the Spirit of the Lord. The sooner we allow God to train us in the little things, the sooner He will give us bigger jobs to do. I know we think we're all ready to go out but we aren't quite ready yet. We think we are. Maybe we have to peel a few more potatoes, or scrub a few more floors or wash a few more dishes. Whatever it is that God is training you in to prepare you, the most important is shedding the old and allowing God's love to come inside of us. We're not going to be envious and jealous of one another, neither are we going to bite and devour one another but we have to walk in His love.

It seems like every once in a while we kind of need to be remembering that Jesus loves us. But this love which He gives to us is not for us. What is it for? If we keep it, it's not any good to us. What do we have to do? Give it away. How do we give it? By going to church on Sunday? No. There's only one way, through brotherly kindness. If you have a brother in need, this ministry is a great example of God's love. Now we did not do it, God did it.

Today, great and mighty things are happening and we have a part in it. You have a part in it. God didn't call you here just to be here. He called you to do whatever He needs to do, He called you to fill you with His love and compassion, to change our lives so that we can reach out to the needs of others.

V. We're Under A New Law, The Law Of His Love

We're under a new law, the law of His love – a new life in Christ Jesus. I think this morning we need to take hold of it.

Sometimes we're so wrapped up in ourselves that we miss it. God wants us to look beyond ourselves. You know the devil said to me one time, "How are you going to minister to people, look at your life." I said, "I'm very aware of it Satan." I got up in the middle of the floor and I stomped my feet at him and I said, "Devil, I'm going to obey the Lord, I'm going to minister to people and God's going to take care of me!" He never bothered me again with it because one thing he knew for sure, I meant business and he wasn't going to stop me. He knew I wasn't going to listen to him. I took a stand. I took a stand and I meant every word of it.

Now we can be determined to allow God to train us to flow by His Spirit and in His love and to bring that love to the world. It isn't how we handle it, it's how we allow Him, He is going to do it. Amen. We may use our psychology or philosophy but it isn't going to work. The only way that's going to work… is His love. **God's love is going to do it.**

God has to perfect us in that love because when we come to Him with our whole heart and we give our whole life to Him then something happens to us. We come under a new law. One day I was teaching and all at once that second verse jumped right out at me and I never saw it like this before.

1. There is therefore now no condemnation to them which are in Christ Jesus, who walk not after the flesh, but after the Spirit.
2. For the law of the Spirit of life in Christ Jesus hath made me free from the law of sin and death. (Romans 8:1-2)

Hath made us free. It jumped right out at me, after years and years of reading this word and it took hold of me. I said, "Thank You Jesus. We're not under the law of sin and death we're under the new law of the Spirit of life in Christ Jesus." His love in us as we walk in the Spirit we fulfill the things of the spirit.

VI. Only Through Brotherly Kindness Can the World Know His Love

God has given us so much and He wants to prepare us, so that we will walk in the truth, live in the truth, obey the truth and the truth will set us free. **How much do we want of Him?** How much do we want to walk by His Spirit?

I would suggest you read this today if you have a minute. Let it penetrate through you. Then get a determination that you're not going to walk in the flesh but you're going to walk in the Spirit so that the Lord can use you to minister His love to the world out there. It's real, it's mighty, and it's wonderful. We have to give our all to Him. If we give our all to Him He gives His all to us. It's up to us. Praise God for His love, for the marvelous provision of that love that we have to give it, we have to share it. It's so wonderful the provision that God has made for us inside.

There's a scripture in II Peter that tells us about how He processes our life to bring His love into our life. The processing brings us into godliness, and after godliness it brings us into brotherly kindness, and after brotherly kindness He brings us into His love. The transforming of our life. I said "Lord, why is brotherly kindness named here?"

He said "Only through brotherly kindness can the world know His love."

Isaiah 58 is the demonstration of the kingdom of God and His love. When He gives us the revelation, it changes our life. Through this demonstration of God's love, men and women come to God. It's not what we do; it's what He does through the changing of our lives. Are we willing to let Him do it or are we going to let our flesh arise and hinder? If we let our flesh die and really allow Him to change our life then we're going to see some marvelous things happen, some things we've never seen in all our life. God is revealing mighty things in this hour to change the lives of the multitudes. They're simple things. They're not the bright things that we would think of. **They're things we would never think of that God is using to change lives.** The simple things, the simple words that He would say that we would not think of, God is bringing forth through a people to set others free.

VII. He Will Rejoice Over Thee With Singing

What a mighty God we serve! The Lord Thy God in the midst of thee is mighty. He will save, He will rejoice over thee with joy. He will rest in His love and He will joy over thee with what? Singing! (Zephaniah 3:17)

Would you like to have the Lord sing to you? I was struck with awe as I read that scripture and I said "God, that You would sing to me?" We're talking about singing to Him but He wants to sing to us.

I was going through an experience, in fact, I was dying in a hospital when the Lord gave me that scripture. As the doctors gave me up, the Lord gave me that scripture. It's awesome to know God is singing to you. He loves you so much because you love Him, because you obey Him, He wants to sing to you and let you know how much He loves you. The doctors gave me up and the devil came to snatch my life.

Every time he came to snatch my life, the Lord gave me that scripture. The Lord thy God in the midst of thee is mighty. He gave me the whole verse not just the first part of it, but all of it. I recognized that He had the power over the devil and that it wasn't my time to go, He brought life back into my body. God wants us to get close to Him so that He can demonstrate His love to us. We're not worthy, but **we're not going on our worthiness, we're going on His love.** That's our privilege to allow the Lord to fill us with His love.

Closing Prayer

Father, we thank You. We thank You for Your love, Jesus. We thank You for the Spirit of God. Lord we pray that even today You have enlightened our understanding that we might come a little closer and allow You to remove the works of the flesh from our lives. That we might be a light unto others and that they may know that you love them.

We thank you for the Living Word. We thank You for the written word. We thank you Jesus that You placed Your love within us by Your Spirit that we might walk in it, live in it, move in it and Lord through Your love others are won to You. We give You glory. Lord let Your blessings come to each and every one of us, cause us to desire to be filled with Your love, compassion, Your gentleness and Your kindness.

We ask this in Your wonderful name Jesus and for Your glory. Amen.

Message by Rev. Agnes I. Numer

REVIEW: FAITH WORKETH BY LOVE

1. "Stand fast therefore in the _____ wherewith Christ hath made us free, and be not entangled again with the yoke of bondage." (Galatians 5:1)
2. We're made _____ in Christ.
3. His _____ isn't going to change so we have to change.
4. God has a way by His Spirit that He wants to lead us not under the _____ but by grace.
5. When we walk in His Spirit the word says we don't fulfill the things of the _____.
6. In your heart you have to have a _____ that you're going to separate yourself from that flesh.
7. We have a new law in us and that law is the law of the Spirit of life in _____.
8. When we're _____ _____ the Bible says the "old man" is buried.
9. We're coming up a new _____, a new creation with a new life in us and the old things pass away.

10. If you live in the Spirit then you _____ in the spirit.
11. God said, we have to bring the spiritual into the natural and the natural into the _____.
12. The love of God is what's going to _____ the lives of the people.
13. He is _____ us to flow by His Spirit.

True or False

14. ___ The love which God gives us is for us alone.
15. ___ God wants us to look beyond ourselves.
16. ___ As we walk in the flesh we fulfill the things of the spirit.

17. _____ is the demonstration of the kingdom of God and His love.
a. Revelation 1
b. Mark 2
c. Isaiah 58

18. It's not what we do; it's what He does through the _____ of our lives.
a. redeeming
b. changing
c. judgment

19. "The Lord thy God in the midst of thee is _____; He will save, He will rejoice over thee with joy; He will rest

in His love; He will joy over thee with singing." (Zephaniah 3:17)
a. powerful
b. holy
c. mighty

20. He transforms us so we can be a _____.
a. light
b. disciple
c. joy

CHAPTER 9
THE PLUMBLINE

THE PLUMBLINE – **It is Time to Make a Decision - We All Have a Choice**

We thank you God for your authority and your love, we thank you for your justice and your mercy. Precious Lord, I thank you to put into our hearts the training that you have for us. Lord we thank you now that the principalities have to go. These powers of hell have to go. We need to line up according to the word of God, filled with Your love and compassion. Lord, You brought us here to train us, we belong to You. We aren't going to allow a defiant spirit to rule in our hearts. So Lord, I thank You to take dominion over every child, man and woman. We give You glory for it Jesus in Your wonderful name. Amen.

Let's Read Psalm 4-7

Psalm 4:1 Hear me when I call, O God of my righteousness: thou hast enlarged me [when I was] in distress; have mercy upon me, and hear my prayer.

Psalm 5:1 Give ear to my words, O LORD, consider my

meditation. 2 Hearken unto the voice of my cry, my King, and my God: for unto thee will I pray. 3 My voice shalt thou hear in the morning, O LORD; in the morning will I direct [my prayer] unto thee, and will look up.

Psalm 6:1 O LORD, rebuke me not in thine anger, neither chasten me in thy hot displeasure. 2 Have mercy upon me, O LORD; for I [am] weak: O LORD, heal me; for my bones are vexed

8 Depart from me, all ye workers of iniquity; for the LORD hath heard the voice of my weeping. 9 The LORD hath heard my supplication; the LORD will receive my prayer. 10 Let all mine enemies be ashamed and sore vexed: let them return [and] be ashamed suddenly.

Psalms 7:1 O LORD my God, in thee do I put my trust: save me from all them that persecute me, and deliver me:

8 The LORD shall judge the people: judge me, O LORD, according to my righteousness, and according to mine integrity [that is] in me. Praise the Lord.

First we must call upon Him. We ask Him to enlarge us and have mercy upon us and hear our prayer. God is telling us what to do so that we can hear Him. We often wonder if He hears our prayers. But when we realize He has set the godly apart for Himself, then we know that He hears us when we pray.

Our committal to God has to come first. We come to Him with a broken and contrite heart, we come with an open mind, we ask for forgiveness and we repent for all the things that we have done. **Then, He hears our prayer,** then He forgives our sins, then He blots them out. **God wants us to know that He hears us** when we call and He will answer as He "gives ear" to our words. God recognizes that we love

Him; in the wee hours of the night, we can commune with Him on our bed.

We hear of people who have to go and have to spend a lot of time alone. You know if God is in us we aren't alone are we? If He's inside of us, you don't have to go somewhere else to talk to Him. You don't have to go out into the field and talk to Him; you can have the privilege of speaking to Him on your bed. **God wants us to know Him. He wants to have that intimate relationship** with us and He's telling us this in Psalm 4. With your own heart, upon your own bed, be still, the Lord talks to us in the wee hours of the morning. He wakes us up at 3 and 4 in the morning. If He's in you, you don't have to go off somewhere else, you just talk to Him and He'll give your answers and He'll lead you by His spirit.

One time a lady came to my house and she said the Lord sent me to take you to my house so the Lord can talk to you. That was new to me, because the Lord talked to me at the clothes line, kitchen sink, scrubbing floors, running the vacuum, making beds, I didn't have to go anywhere else. The Lord said to me, "I didn't send her to tell you to go to her house. If you had gone to her house and spent the night so I could talk to you, it wouldn't have been me talking to you because I talk to you everywhere." **God wants us to have an intimate relationship with Him.**

Remember, He does hear our prayers. He forgives our sins and cleanses us from all unrighteousness. And what a joy it is to know that we have peace, that we can lay down in peace and sleep and dwell in safety. God has called us to a life of peace and rest; we have to give our life to the Lord in **total commitment to Him.** God will not meet our needs half way and we can't come half way to Him, we have to come all the way, He **requires total surrender.**

Let me tell you, it's kind of one sided... What is He taking away from us? He is taking away sin and darkness; evil habits, alcohol, drugs, all of the lust of the flesh and the pride of the flesh. He's taking it all away and you are free. Then why do you look back and let the devil torment your mind instead of speaking I'm free, I'm free? The Lord has set me free.

A young woman came from Kansas that had a lot of principalities and powers in her life. She ran away down the road. The young people went to rescue her because anyone could pick her up and it was pretty evil out there. As the young people ran to get to her, a very tall angel dressed in white, ran after her and tripped her. They caught up with her and brought her back. This young woman was warring against deliverance and decided she would run away again. This time a drunken man picked her up and took her to a place where a lot of evil activity was going on. She got away from him and called home. She could have been killed very quickly but we were interceding for her ever since she walked out the door.

God has a way for you that is His peace, His righteousness, His forgiveness and His healing. We can't play with God or with the devil because the devil will sure trip you and pull you down fast. Peace comes from God, Joy comes from God, Salvation comes from Him, Love comes from Him. The Lord is calling us into this very beautiful relationship He's talking about in Psalm 4. God's presence and Love in us. **God wants us to put our trust in Him.** We all trust our flesh but do we trust God? You are a chosen people and God has chosen you to be 100% in Him, He will train you so He can be 100% in you out there against the evil of this world.

You will never know unless you put your trust in Him and let Him show you that He is God.

We can do our own thing and God won't stop us because He honors your right to choose. The Lord taught me some 40 years ago that I have no right to interfere with the choice that anyone is making. I have to stand back and let them make it, because they have the right to make it whether it is right or wrong. Sometimes the Holy Ghost says to me "I'm drawing the plumbline and this is the last time I'm coming this way." When He says that, I have to obey Him and He has done it.

There was a man I knew who had a wife and two children. They used to come to us for help. One night, in the middle of the night, he came for deliverance. He had principalities and powers in his life that were very evil. So we prayed and fasted for Him and the Lord delivered him. His wife, well she wasn't too concerned about God, she said that when she needed Him, she would think of Him.

One day the Lord told me to go to their house. The Lord told me I want you to go to that home and I want you to read this scripture to them.

Amos 7:6 The Lord repented for this: This also shall not be, saith the Lord God. 7 Thus he shewed me: and, behold, the Lord stood upon a wall made by a plumbline, with a **plumbline in his hand.** 8 And the Lord said unto me, Amos, what seest thou? And I said, A plumbline. Then said the Lord, Behold, I will set a plumbline in the midst of my people Israel: I will not again pass by them any more:

I went that night and the Lord gave them the word. My son said to his wife, "Do you know something about the Lord?" She said, "I think of the Lord, when I need Him." He said "What?" I thought this was awful strange that she had no communication with God at all. So that night after we left the husband walked out of that house never to return again. He divorced his wife and went his own way and married someone else. Sometime later, he was in a motorcycle accident and ended up in the intensive care unit in the hospital. I went to talk to him and believe he had made his peace with God before he passed away.

His wife, well, she wasn't going the way God wanted her to because she had no interest in God... except when she needed Him. Five years later, the wife called me in the middle of the night and said her son was crossing the street at about 3 in the morning and a truck hit him and killed him instantly... the little boy had died, just like his father. I knew the boy in diapers. When he was about 8 years old, he carried a Bible around and said I'm going to be a preacher. He loved the Lord, but years went by and now he was 16 years old. He had joined with some devil worshipers, all of his friends were devil worshipers. When we went to the mortuary, his friends were very sad. We said, "Do you know that this boy didn't make it to God? He made a choice and joined the gangs and lost his life without God." They said, "Not our friend, this couldn't happen to him." He said, "Do you know your friend is in hell now?" "Not our friend..." "Yes, your friend, because he chose evil rather than the good." I prayed for some of his friends, they were all dressed in black; they didn't look like human beings. It was so terrible. All I could think of was this little boy ...with a Bible.

We are responsible to bring our children up in the ways of the Lord. You cannot have God in your life and decide you are going to run your own life, because as surely as you live, you are going to meet up with death and you are going to lose it. When God has called us to His way, and we choose our own way... there is trouble.

Little did I know that night that He gave the word that God had put the plumbline down and wasn't going to go that way anymore. Little did I know what was going to happen to that entire family. **We have choices to make.** God will not stop you from your own way, but your own way will take you away from God.

We must ask Him to take out of us everything that is contrary to His perfect will and to put His love in us **until everything in us is filled with His love.** It is up to us to choose, because God made us free. He won't interfere... we have a choice to make.

I was in Africa in a village and I met a business man who God had blessed but then he became greedy. He wasn't satisfied with the blessings of the Lord. He told the Lord he had some deals with people and the Lord told him it was bribery. He didn't think it was bribery, he thought it was just his friends.

This businessman told us a story. Monday, the Lord said to him to get his house in order because on Saturday he was going to die. God said, "I'm not finished with you." This was Monday and the Lord He told him "You get everything straight and ask everyone to forgive you." The businessman remembered one woman that had a lot of hate against him. He went to see her and said, "I want you to forgive me." She threw hot soup in his face. He wondered what he was going to do. Eventually he got her to listen and forgive him. He only had one week to save his life. God said, "Get your house in order." On Saturday he was healthy there was nothing wrong with him, but he died.

Sunday morning, his family brought him to the His Stripes Hospital... dead. A corpse... there was nothing they could do; they didn't have time for a corpse. The doctor had heard the story of Lazarus in his Sunday school class as he listened the Lord said, "You take this corpse and bring him to your hospital." His head nurse said, "This man's dead, he's a corpse." "Put an IV in him." "He doesn't have any veins." The doctor said, "Put it where you know the veins are." He was dead for four days. The head nurse put him in the bed as the doctor ordered. The doctor went home to rest for a little while, he felt very tired and fell asleep then the Lord took him by the Spirit to follow the businessman that had died.

The businessman went into the heavens. They open up the book of life to see if his name was written in it. God said, "I have four counts against you." So, they came with a bottle and a brush, in that bottle was the blood of Jesus. They took that brush and washed away the four charges against him. He stood there and didn't know what was going to happen because he wasn't sure the Lord had forgiven him. The Lord washed it away right in front of him.

The businessman sees a friend behind him who was a Christian and he hears them say, "Depart from me I never knew you." Others came and He said, "Depart from me I never knew you." When he got to a certain point and the Lord told him, "You have to go back." The doctor heard what the Lord was saying to this man. The Lord took him back to his bedroom. The doctor waited for the businessman to return. Every day, he thought he would come back and find this man awake but it wasn't so... four days went by. On the fourth day, there were tears coming down his eye. That was the first sign of life. The Lord restored him for one purpose, God said, "Go and tell my people there's no purgatory. There's heaven and hell. You choose one or the other, go and warn my people."

Choices we make determine where we are going to live for eternity.

There's only two places to go. When I was 16, I'd gone so far away from God that the Lord shook me over hell. He opened hell up and He said to me, "If you don't serve me, that is where you will go." And that's as straight as it is. If we don't serve Him, that's where we're going to go.

But think of what God is going to give to us in exchange. How can we resist His love, and that which He has given to us? Do we prefer darkness in our life? He can send us to hell or are we willing to let Him clean our house and fill us with His love until our being is saturated with the love of God. I'm not a hell fire preacher but I know very well what hell is like. I know the price that we have to pay if we don't walk with God with all our heart.

The people who don't want to help the poor, one day before very long are going to stand before God. God is not going to ask them how many thousands of souls they have brought into the kingdom. He is going to ask "I was hungry and you fed Me not, I was thirsty and you gave Me no drink. I was a stranger and you took Me not in, naked and you clothed Me not. I was sick and you visited Me not, I was in prison and ye came not to Me." I don't care how big we are, if we're not doing the command of the Lord we're going to miss it.

Isaiah 58 is very loud and clear and God requires it of us Maybe you don't want to do it, but **if you love God it's in your heart to meet the needs of others.** There's only one outlet on this earth and that is brotherly kindness... loving one another, serving one another, helping the poor, meeting the needs that Jesus laid before us in the Gospels. That which Jesus did, He requires of us to do.

We have a straight line – a plumbline. I don't mind walking that line, because it's a line of peace, joy, righteousness and holiness with the Lord. We need this understanding. God is calling a people who He can love and sing to, who He can rejoice over, as we walk and run in His love to the nations of the world. What God has in store for us is very awesome as we empty out ourselves and let His love fill us.

In the story of the businessman, the one thing that was missing with a woman that was sent to hell was that she didn't have God's love. That was the only thing that was against her. If the love of the world is in us, then the love of the Father isn't. If we love the Father, the love of the world isn't in us. God is drawing a straight line in our lives, so He can fill us and His love will flow through us.

God will make the way for us, we don't have to make it for ourselves and if we make it for ourselves we are going to miss it. If we give our way to God, God will direct it and we will have that peace, joy and righteousness. It's better to have Jesus in charge of our life. **It is better to have His love and glory and His kingdom operating in us.**

We have a choice to make. If we chose Him we shall eternally be blessed by Him and live in His kingdom forever. If we don't choose Him we will be damned forever. It's not a little thing... we need to choose Him. He loves us; He doesn't want us to go to the place where the devil is going. He wants us to go to the place that He has chosen for us. He won't force us or compel us, except by His love to draw us unto Him. His love compels us to follow Him.

I want to leave these words with you, **choose Him, there isn't anything lacking in what He wants for us if we will but follow Him.** God has given us so much, if we will just hear what He's saying, we don't have to entangle ourselves with other things and it's so clear and simple and mighty, if we receive it.

God will impart it to you if you allow Him. Be willing to walk that path of liberty, peace and joy, righteousness and holiness.

Father we thank You for this word. Jesus we thank you that you don't say one thing and do another, neither do you want us saying one thing and doing something else. Lord speak to our hearts, let us know your great love and provision that you might take this Gospel of the Kingdom of Jesus Christ into all the world, that we might be a witness to all nations. So that you Lord can return again unto your people. Lord Jesus, speak your love, your comfort and your strength to us. Lord let your spirit flow through us moving in our lives, so that we choose to walk in the Spirit of Life. Lord Jesus, bring life that we may live throughout all eternity. We rejoice in everything you have done for us, for you said you will not hold anyone guiltless who turned away from Christ or rejected Him. Lord we thank you for the truth and the truth will make us free. Jesus, I thank you for ears to hear and a heart to receive and a heart to obey, in Jesus name Amen.

Taken from the message "The Plumbline – It is Time to Make a Decision - We All Have a Choice" by Rev. Agnes I. Numer

REVIEW: THE PLUMBLINE

Discussion questions

1. Do we have to be in a certain special place to talk with God? Where do you talk with Him?
2. What does God require from us? The Lord is calling us into a very close relationship. Describe your relationship with God.
3. What is a plumbline?
4. What is it used for?
5. What does it mean when God sets a plumbline in our lives?
6. If we do not serve God with all of our heart what will happen to us?
7. What are the joys of serving God and walking "a straight line"?
8. What path must be willing to walk?

Review:

1. Amos 7:7 …the Lord stood upon a wall made by a plumbline, with a _____ in his hand. 8 And the Lord said unto me, Amos, what seest thou? And I said, A _____. Then said the Lord, Behold, I will set a _____ in the midst of my _____ Israel:

2. God has called us to a life of peace and rest. We have to give our life to the _____ in total _____ to Him. He requires _____ _____.

3. Peace comes from God, _____ comes from God, _____ comes from Him, _____ comes from Him. God wants us to put our _____ in Him.

4. _____ determine where we are going to _____ for eternity.

5. If we choose Him, we shall eternally _____ be blessed by him and live in his kingdom forever if we don't not choose Him, we will be damned forever.
a. True
b. False

6. God will impart it to you if you _____Him. Be _____ to walk the path of _____, peace and joy, _____ and holiness.

7. There is only one _____, and that is brotherly _____, loving one another, _____ one another, helping the poor, meeting the _____ that Jesus laid before us in the _____. That which Jesus _____, He _____ of us to do.

CHAPTER 10
THE VISION STATEMENT

EVERY MINISTRY MUST HAVE a Vision Statement that clearly states your primary goal. You must also have a Mission Statement that states your core purpose and focus.

Definition: Vision Statement - A one-sentence statement describing the clear and inspirational long-term desired change resulting from an organization or program's work.

Here are some examples:

- Oxfam: A just world without poverty (5 words)
- Habitat for Humanity: A world where everyone has a decent place to live. (10)
- NPR, with its network of independent member stations, is America's pre-eminent news institution (12)
- World Vision: For every child, life in all its fullness; Our prayer for every heart, the will to make it so (19)

- In Touch Ministries: proclaiming the Gospel of Jesus Christ to people in every country of the world. (14)
- Mission Statement - what you do: A one-sentence statement describing the reason an organization or program exists. It is used to help guide decisions about priorities, actions, and responsibilities. Here are some examples:
- TED: Spreading Ideas. (2 words)
- Smithsonian: The increase and diffusion of knowledge. (6 words)
- Livestrong: To inspire and empower people affected by cancer. (8)
- Charity water: We're a non-profit organization bringing clean, safe drinking water to people in developing countries. (14)
- In Touch Ministries: To lead people worldwide into a growing relationship with Jesus Christ and to strengthen the local church. (17)

God's vision has always been clearly defined and communicated to Israel.

God made a covenant starting with Abraham, "I will be your God and you will be my people" God declared that He would have a people in the earth who will show forth His praise.

There are **three main promises** in the covenant made with Abraham and his descendants.

1. The **promise of land** (Genesis 12:1). God called Abraham from Ur of the Chaldees to a land that

He would give him (Genesis 12:1). This promise is reiterated in Genesis 13:14–18 where it is confirmed by a shoe covenant; its dimensions are given in Genesis 15:18–21. See also Deuteronomy 30:1–10, the Palestinian Covenant.

2. The **promise of descendants** (Genesis 12:2). God promised Abraham that He would make a great nation out of him. Abraham, who was 75 years old and childless (Genesis 12:4), was promised many descendants. In Genesis 17:6 nations and kings his descendants. Even the promised Messiah would come through his offspring.

3. The **promise of blessing and redemption** (Genesis 12:3). God promised to bless Abraham and the families of the earth through him. This promise is amplified in the New Covenant (Jeremiah 31:31–34; Hebrews 8:6–13) and has to do with Israel's spiritual blessing and redemption. Jeremiah anticipates the forgiveness of sin. Reaffirmed to Isaac (Genesis 21:12;26:3–4). Confirmed to Jacob (Genesis 28:14–15).

There is coming a day when Israel as a nation will be converted, forgiven, and restored (Romans 11:25–27) when Israel will repent and receive the forgiveness of God (Zechariah 12:10–14). It is through the nation Israel that God promised in Genesis 12:1–3 to bless the nations of the world. That ultimate blessing will result in their forgiveness of sins and Messiah's glorious kingdom reign on earth.

Jesus stated His mission before He started His ministry. After being baptized Jesus went into the wilderness to be tempted by the devil. When He came out victorious He stood in a synagogue and read this verse:

Luke 4:18 "The Spirit of the Lord is upon me, because he anointed me to preach the gospel to the poor. He has sent me to proclaim release to the captives, and recovery of sight to the blind, to set free those who are oppressed...

God's vision for the Church is for people of every tribe, tongue and nation, to hear the gospel and to become the Bride of Christ. Our Mission Statement is very clearly given to us by Jesus himself through Matthew 25 - preach, baptize and teach all peoples in all nations.

And he said to them, "Go into all the world and proclaim the gospel to the whole creation". Mark 16:15 ESV

Go therefore and make disciples of all nations, baptizing them in the name of the Father and of the Son and of the Holy Spirit, Matthew 28:19 (ESV)

Unity of Vision

One of the greatest challenges is that there are often different visions within a congregation. Please see examples below.

God's Vision - the purpose God has called that particular group together. He has a plan, purpose and vision that is a part of the "Greater Plan"

The **Pastor's Vision** - when a pastor has heard from the Holy Spirit he will have some idea of God's plan for that congregation.

A leader has his own ideas or training and he has his own agenda as well.

The People's Vision. Both the congregation and its core of leaders have a vision.

The elders surrounding the Pastor may want to share and have input in the overall vision. They may know the history better than the Pastor.

These people may have a certain identity of their own from past leaders and experiences.

Some people are self-serving or indifferent.

Some people may have received past teaching that may affect their vision for their church.

Clear Vision Encourages Unity

A clear, shared vision encourages and allows people to come together and work together. It creates a common identity and mutual goals. It allows people to "climb on board— let us go together". It also gives people a purpose in what they do because they are an important part of something which is going somewhere. A common vision says that we are working together toward the same goals. We need each other!

Bringing your congregation into unity of vision.

Once you have established the clear vision of what God wants to bring about in your ministry, how can you now share this vision and bring the people into a unity of purpose. Remember that **people usually resist change.**

Use the following steps to help bring your congregation into unity of vision:

1. Prepare yourself. Prayerfully seek and know God's vision.

2. Develop trust relationships with your core leaders so that they may also have an input on the vision.
3. Pray together. Seek God. Discuss the vision together.
4. When possible go on a retreat with your leaders and pray about the vision.
5. Set long term and short term goals.

Once your core leadership shares the same vision… now it's time to:

- Call a meeting.
- Have a "Reality Check". Realistically, where are we right now? Really.
- What challenges are we facing, where are we really going? Do we know our purpose?
- Share the vision, with everyone, make it plain. Say "This is where we, all the core leaders, believe God is leading us."
- All core leaders are united, they are sitting together and various ones are sharing in support of "our vision".
- Communication is a two way street and we need to allow input. People who feel that their input is **heard** will likely give their best to fulfill the vision.
- Unless it also becomes their vision, you will be pushing uphill all the way.

- **Repeat, repeat, repeat.** It is important to continually emphasize the importance of the vision.
- Use slogans, bywords and even name changes. Put the vision in the bulletin, on posters and whatever is appropriate.
- Pray together for specific milestones to be reached and needs to be met.
- **Celebrate small milestones** and keep up the enthusiasm.
- **Remember to say "Thank you."** Always recognize a job well done.

Here are some scriptures about vision:

Thus says the Lord of hosts: "Do not listen to the words of the prophets who prophesy to you, filling you with vain hopes. They speak visions of their own minds, not from the mouth of the Lord. Jeremiah 23:16 ESV

Where there is no prophetic vision the people cast off restraint, but blessed is he who keeps the law. Proverbs 29:18 ESV

For still the vision awaits its appointed time; it hastens to the end—it will not lie. If it seems slow, wait for it; it will surely come; it will not delay. Habakkuk 2:3 ESV

And the Lord answered me: "Write the vision; make it plain on tablets, so he may run who reads it. Habakkuk 2:2 ESV

For I know the plans I have for you, declares the Lord, plans for welfare and not for evil, to give you a future and a hope. Jeremiah 29:11 ESV

For the Lord God does nothing without revealing his secret to his servants the prophets. Amos 3:7 ESV

In ministry and in business we need to have a **clear view of our Vision**, and we need to know "**who we are and what we do**" which will give us a **strong unity of purpose.**

REVIEW: THE VISION STATEMENT

1. A vision statement clearly states your primary goal
a. T
b. F

2. The vision statement should be one paragraph that explains your ministry
a. T
b. F

3. The mission statement tells what your ministry particularly does
a. T
b. F

4. I will be your God and you will be my people is God's stated vision for who?
a. David
b. Noah

c. Jesus
d. Abraham

5. Jesus stated his mission which is found in which scripture
a. John 17:17
b. Luke 4
c. Psalms 23
d. Revelation 20:10

6. What is God's vision for the church?
a. To conquer the whole world for God
b. People from everywhere would have the opportunity to hear the gospel and become Christ's Bride
c. That all His people would become prosperous and healthy

7. The Mission God gave us was to:
a. Preach, baptize and Teach all nations
b. Diligently study his word daily
c. Live a life separated and consecrated to Him

8. The people in a congregation may have their own vision for their church
a. True
b. False

9. A clear shared vision creates
a. An atmosphere where people can work together
b. Unity of purpose
c. A sense of importance in the people in the congregation
d. All of the above

10. To bring a congregation into unity of purpose the pastor must know Gods vision for his church
a. T
b. F

CHAPTER 11
PRAISE AND WORSHIP

Before beginning this course please review Basic Foundations Chapter 1 - Who is God?

Singing without God's anointing – is just singing.

"It is a fearful thing to produce "Praise and Worship" music that leads into hunger for more music – worship must lead to a hunger for the depths of God and His word. As worship leaders we are taking the chance that the general public may or may not like the music that God prophesies through us...but it is more important to please God. We know the place that the enemy had was to bring praises before the throne. How careful we must be that we will not fall like he did and long for that praise for ourselves."

In the old testament the Holy of Holies was hidden by a veil. The only time anyone was allowed to enter was once a year on the Holy Day Yom Kippur. Only the High Priest entered and offered blood sacrifices and burned incense before the Mercy Seat.

. . .

TODAY, AS MUSICIANS WE ARE ALSO CONSIDERED PRIESTS.

Why do we want to enter the Holy of Holies?

The office of the priest was a hereditary role. The priest spent his entire life serving God and offering sacrifices to ask forgiveness for God's people. Some priests were the most wicked men in the nation, instead of crying out against sin, they joined into sin. As musicians let us guard our hearts, that we may carry God's presence to His people that they may come into His presence for healing, restoration and the forgiveness of sin. Let us praise and worship with a pure heart without shame and without shaming God.

Before the priest went into the Holy of Holies he sanctified himself. He set himself aside and asked God to cleanse him from his sin and remove anything that would offend God. Sanctification identifies us with God, who is separate from this world. The priest wore special garments with beautiful colors with gold, blue, purple and scarlet.

May we see the Worship Leader as a priest before God?

Who is the Worshiper?

The worshiper is not only those singing in front. The people we sing to will also worship God. We do not bring others into the presence of God. We worship God and as His presence fills the room, people choose to enter or do not choose to enter in.

Leading Worship

As a worship leader we discern the Heart of our Father God and praise Him – as we worship God, God brings His people into His presence and He compels our hearts into a deeper commitment.

As worship leaders our devotion to God and our love for God shows through our worship. We cannot pretend, our skill can hide how deep our relationship is with God. It is to that extent that we will express worship.

Why do we want to enter into God's intimate presence?

So that they will long to live there – forever, forsaking sin and all other gods. Desiring to be the bride of Christ, not just remaining a disciple. That their hearts may become open to receive the rest of the service, the word of God through the Pastor or the ministry that will be given after the song service.

As we chose to worship, God strengthens us to pass through everything.

Remember Paul singing in prison?

And when they had laid many stripes upon them, they cast [them] into prison, charging the jailor to keep them safely: 24 Who, having received such a charge, thrust them into the inner prison, and made their feet fast in the stocks.

25 And at midnight Paul and Silas prayed, and sang praises unto God: and the prisoners heard them. Acts 16:23-25.

Man is made with a soul, a spirit and our body. Our soul consists of our mind, will and emotions. Our spirit comes from God and relates to God. Our body is where we live. This helps us to understand how we worship.

There are different realms of Praise and Worship.

The Soulish Realm

Music can move people. It moves people to dance, to sing, to "fall in love," to be depressed, to be happy.

Most music is performed in the soulish realm. Its purpose is to entertain. But does this music compel our hearts to enter into God's presence?

The Realm of Praise

Praise begins to minister to the Spirit man. This music begins to compel the heart to focus on God rather than self. The Spirit of God begins to move in the hearts of people, He may bring healing, deliverance and other gifts of the Spirit.

Praise ye the LORD. Sing unto the LORD a new song, [and] his praise in the congregation of saints. 2 Let Israel rejoice in him that made him let the children of Zion be joyful in their King. 3 Let them praise his name in the dance let them sing praises unto him with the timbrel and harp. 4 For the LORD taketh pleasure in his people he will beautify the meek with salvation. 5 Let the saints be joyful in glory let them sing aloud upon their beds. Psalms 149:1-5

The Realm of Worship

When the worship leader discerns the Heart of the God and worships Him, **God brings His people into His presence.**

When we enter into God's presence through worship our lives change. We enter into His presence abandoning our worries, concerns and appointments, our focus is on God alone. We realize God's greatness, His love and who He is. It is in this place that God speaks to our hearts giving us healing, direction and peace. It is in this realm that we become so aware of Him.

We cannot be afraid to enter into intimate worship of God in front of others. It is only by entering into this place of intimate worship that we can lead others to the freedom of expressing their love to their Heavenly Father.

Praise in Spiritual Warfare

When we look at King Jehoshaphat we see an incredible situation:

And when they began to sing and to praise, the LORD set ambushments against the children of Ammon, Moab, and mount Seir, which were come against Judah; and they were smitten. 2 Chronicles 20:22

We see here that as God's people not just sang but praised Him, He destroyed the enemy. There are times that God uses our praise as Spiritual Warfare – when we sing the enemy flees.

6 [Let] the high [praises] of God [be] in their mouth and a twoedged sword in their hand; 7 To execute vengeance upon the heathen, [and] punishments upon the people; 8 To bind their kings with chains, and their nobles with fetters of iron; 9 To execute upon them the judgment written this honour have all his saints. Praise ye the LORD. Psalm 149:6-9

Which realm does the music you play and the songs that you sing lead those listening into?

A good guideline for praise and worship is to realize that we are only accompanying what God is doing.

We must realize that we are created to praise God.

We come before Him with a pure heart.

Come expecting God to move.

As God moves flow with Him.

Our responsibility is to compliment God not to expect God to assist us.

We are priests before Him. Worship Him in spirit and in

truth not bringing shame to Him but bringing His people before Him that He may remove their shame.

Anticipate that God will move among His people He inhabits the praises of His people and when God moves - we change.

Worship God in Spirit and in truth. Purify your heart before you start playing. Bring your praise as an offering before Him. If you have any sin, or anything against anyone take care of it before you worship. Ask for forgiveness clear the disagreement. That you may be a priest before Him.

Practice **before you play**. Practice your instrument, practice playing and singing as a group. Make sure that those engineering your team have all of the amplification equipment ready before you worship. Don't allow team members to practice during worship. We do not want to be a distraction - we want to worship God.

The focus is on God not on ourselves.

Praise ye the LORD. Praise God in his sanctuary: praise him in the firmament of his power. 2 Praise him for his mighty acts: praise him according to his excellent greatness. 3 Praise him with the sound of the trumpet: praise him with the psaltery and harp. 4 Praise him with the timbrel and dance: praise him with stringed instruments and organs. 5 Praise him upon the loud cymbals: praise him upon the high sounding cymbals. 6 Let every thing that hath breath praise the LORD. **Praise ye the LORD.** Psalms 150:1-6

REVIEW: PRAISE AND WORSHIP

1. Singing without God's anointing – is just singing.
a. True
b. False

2. Musicians are not considered priests.
a. True
b. False

3. Lucifer used to bring praises before the throne.
a. True
b. False

4. As musicians let us _____ our hearts, that we may carry God's _____ to His people that they may receive _____, _____ and the forgiveness of sin.

5. Let us praise and worship with a _____ _____ without _____ and without shaming God.

6. Before the priest went into the Holy of Holies, he sanctified himself. Should we sanctify ourselves before worship?
a. Yes
b. No
c. Sometimes

7. Our love for God shows through our worship
a. True
b. False

8. We can pretend, our skill will hide how deep our relationship is with God.
a. True
b. False

9. As we _____ to worship, God _____ us to pass through everything.

10. Which realm is not a realm of Praise and Worship?
a. Praise in Spiritual Warfare
b. Realm of Dreams
c. Soulish Realm
d. Realm of Worship

11. When singing, how would we make sure we are not a distraction?
a. Practice before you play.
b. Make sure engineer has equipment ready before you start.
c. Don't allow practice during worship.
d. All the above

12. Which is not a guideline that will accompany what God is doing?
a. Realize we are created to praise God.
b. Come before Him with a pure heart.
c. Play with confidence in yourself as a great musician
d. Come desiring God to move.
e. As God moves flow with Him.

13. Our responsibility is to _____ God not to _____ God to _____ us.

14. If the congregation is not singing with us what should we not do?
a. Focus on God
b. Yell at the congregation
c. Play songs that the congregation may know
d. Make sure that the songs are not too high or too low.

CHAPTER 12
COME UP HIGHER IN HIS LOVE

I. Our Human Love Does Not Compare With God's Love

Paul was well pleased with the Philippians, and he loved them very dearly. He states that they were his joy and crown. He said, "So stand fast in the Lord..." He gave instruction to them, but he also is saying to pray: "... in everything by prayer and supplication let your requests be made known unto God. And the peace of God, which passeth all understanding, shall keep your hearts and minds through Christ Jesus." Tonight I believe we need to renew these words in our own life. Here in this place, where we are so close to one another, it's not so easy because some are more processed than others; some have been through the fire a little more – and have a lot of stuff burned out. And some haven't had it yet. Paul was kind of allowing all of this. "And the peace of God, which passeth all understanding, shall keep your hearts and minds through Christ Jesus."

Philippians 4:1-15

1 Therefore, my brethren dearly beloved and longed for, my joy and crown, so stand fast in the Lord, my dearly beloved.

2 I beseech Euodias, and beseech Syntyche, that they be of the same mind in the Lord.

3 And I intreat thee also, true yokefellow, help those women which laboured with me in the gospel, with Clement also, and with other my fellowlabourers, whose names are in the book of life.

4 Rejoice in the Lord always: and again I say, Rejoice.

5 Let your moderation be known unto all men. The Lord is at hand.

6 Be careful for nothing; but in every thing by prayer and supplication with thanksgiving let your requests be made known unto God.

7 And the peace of God, which passeth all understanding, shall keep your hearts and minds through Christ Jesus.

8 Finally, brethren, whatsoever things are true, whatsoever things are honest, whatsoever things are just, whatsoever things are pure, whatsoever things are lovely, whatsoever things are of good report; if there be any virtue, and if there be any praise, think on these things.

9 Those things, which ye have both learned, and received, and heard, and seen in me, do: and the God of peace shall be with you.

10 But I rejoiced in the Lord greatly, that now at the last your care of me hath flourished again; wherein ye were also careful, but ye lacked opportunity.

11 Not that I speak in respect of want: for I have learned, in whatsoever state I am, therewith to be content.

12 I know both how to be abased, and I know how to abound: every where and in all things I am instructed both to be full and to be hungry, both to abound and to suffer need.

13 I can do all things through Christ which strengtheneth me.

14 Notwithstanding ye have well done, that ye did communicate with my affliction.

15 Now ye Philippians know also, that in the beginning of the gospel, when I departed from Macedonia, no church communicated with me as concerning giving and receiving, but ye only.

God's love is so mighty. He wants to do so much in our life that will change our life. He wants to remove that which is human in nature, and He wants to let God's peace come, and keep our hearts and minds through Him. There are times when we are moved by circumstances; the Lord wants to change us so that we can be like Him. I truly believe that God wants to so transform our lives with His love that we do not have the interference of human love – realizing that God's love surpasses anything else. God is doing the impossible in every one of our lives so that we can go forth in His love and that His love is going to reach the world. I do not believe that human love mixed with God's love is perfect. I believe its imperfect. But what God wants to do for us is to remove the carnal love and put a love for others that we will not be affected by circumstances. For example, if we love somebody, helping someone, and they do something very bad against us, then we are hurt and we go on the defensive. But God is saying, that the peace of God which passeth all understanding, shall keep your hearts and your minds through Jesus Christ.

Let's turn to 1 Corinthians 13 (Amplified Version)

1 Corinthians 13:4-8 says: "Love endures long and is patient and kind; love never is envious nor boils over with jealousy, is not boastful or vainglorious, does not display itself haughtily. It is not conceited, (arrogant and inflated with pride); it is not rude (unmannerly) and does not act unbecomingly. God's love (God's love in us) does not insist on its own rights or its own way, for it is not self-seeking; it is not touchy or fretful or resentful; it takes no account of the evil done to it, (it pays no attention to a suffered wrong). It does not rejoice at injustice and unrighteousness, but rejoices when right and truth prevail. Love bears up under anything and everything that comes; is ever ready to believe the best of every person, its hopes are fadeless under all circumstances, and it endures everything (without weakening). Love never fails, (never fades out or become obsolete or comes to an end). As for prophecy (the gift of interpretation of the divine will and purpose), it will be fulfilled and pass away; as for tongues, they will be destroyed and cease; as for knowledge, it will pass away; (it will lose its value and be superceded by truth)."

We are living in the hour of the Spirit of Truth. I believe the Spirit of Truth is going to take the place of these other things. I believe God is bringing it strong into our lives that we may know the truth – that we may walk in the truth and obey the truth. And He has given us His peace, which is beyond anything that we can understand. Our human love does not compare with God's love. We fail with it. We get affected by it. Our emotions are involved with it, and they get torn up. But if we allow God to remove these things from our lives so that His pure love is in there – His pure love responding to every situation – then we will not be affected by the situation. And I grant you that it's very difficult for us, many times, to be silent when we feel we need to speak out. It's difficult for us not to be angry when situations arise that try us to the limit. God gets angry, too, remember that; but His anger is different than human anger. His anger is different. Our anger has many things that His love does not have. The anger that comes out of us is not God-given, mostly. Sometimes God will come in His anger, but He is saying to us that He wants His love to take the place of this human love that is not good. It's selfish, it's self- centered, it's self-seeking, it's all of these things – it's jealous, it's vainglorious, it's boastful and it gets haughty. But God's love does not do any of that.

II. God Is Perfecting Us With His Love

But, you know you don't learn this overnight. You learn it by processing. We learn it by the processing God is doing in our life. I remember a time in my life when the Lord said to me, "You cannot love your husband, you cannot love your children more than you love the stranger coming out there." Well, that was a pretty big "wallop". How could I do that? I could do that only if I permitted Him to take from me that which is not like Him, not His love. We have love one for another, but it may not be God's love; it may be just a thing we feel one toward another. But when **we have God's love in us, then we feel differently.** God does something that helps us in any situation we don't know how to handle. I can tell you in this place we have trying times. Trying times with one another; trying times with our children; and trying times with ourselves – because we kind of like our own life.

But with God's love in your life, you try to be careful concerning what you say, what you do, how you act. Some of us do not exemplify God's love very much, do we? How many know that? You know that. And sometimes when you don't exemplify His love, teachers get angry, schools get torn up and spirits run everywhere. And then we have to get in and pray, and get rid of it. Well God is perfecting you too, with His love. And **one day you'll be able to stand in a congregation of people, and you will only feel God's love for one another, because He will take everything else out of our life – if we will let Him.**

One thing about the Lord, sometimes we slip up; we say and do things. But just as soon as we do, something happens. How many know that? Pretty soon we're aware that really wasn't the Lord, but it was our own reactions. God is perfecting us in His peace; He's perfecting us in His love. He said all these things are going to pass away, but My love will **never** pass away. My peace will **never** pass away. My joy will never pass away. God wants that under any and all circumstances we rest in His peace, we rest in His love, and we have His joy; **in the midst of all kinds of circumstances, the Lord will keep us.**

He was saying here, "And the peace of God, which passeth all understanding, shall keep your hearts and minds ..." Not just your heart, but your mind. "...through Christ Jesus." These things will not change. Heaven and earth will pass away, but Jesus said "My word shall **NEVER** pass away." And what's He doing in our life is forever. Amen? He's removing from us the hindrances; He's removing from us the things that, if we're trained here to go out to other countries, it's very, very important that we are trained in the little things. It's very important that God's love is what is governing our life. It's very important that His peace is there, and His joy is there. That love, peace and joy which He has imparted to us is going to tell the world out there that Jesus loves them. And this is why we need to allow the Lord to remove the junk out of our lives and let the flesh go, so that we can have His pure love abiding in us.

We do not exemplify God when we go in fits of anger. We do not exemplify Him when we want our own way, doing our own thing. God wants us to come into a relationship with Him, with His pure love and peace and joy, so that we can flow together in whatever God has for us to do. His peace, His love, His joy... I can tell you that I have much more patience, I have much more endurance at 80 years than I had at 40 years. I can tell you that He's done a lot in my life, and He can do the same in yours. It doesn't have to take 40 years to do it. All it takes is a determination to let the Lord change your life. And it can be done quickly, if we really choose to walk in His love, and let go of the human stuff we call love.

III. God's Love Doesn't Expect Anything In Return

We get hurt by our love and it hurts us. God's love doesn't hurt us. God's love doesn't expect anything in return. It's pure – it reaches out and loves everybody without wanting anything in return. If you want something in return, then there must be some of your own desire there and your own love. God is saying, "Don't expect anything from other people. Love them with the love of the Lord, and they will respond with God's love." But if we show anything else, we're hindering what God wants us to do, what He wants us to be. He wants His love to change our life. It's up to us. It's not conceited, it's not arrogant, and it's not inflated with pride. It's not rude. God's love does not insist on its own rights or its own way. For it is not self-seeking, it's not selfish, it's not touchy, it's not fretful and not resentful. It takes no account of the evil done to it. We need that, don't we? We need that because pretty soon, somebody does something to us, and something rises up inside of us in defense.

Many years ago, God was dealing with me, and I said, "But God, I don't deserve that kind of treatment." How many of you have ever said that? "God, I don't deserve that kind of treatment." I was pretty stubborn about it; because I was sure I was right. I was positive I was right, that I didn't deserve that kind of treatment. But God said to me, "You hard head! It doesn't matter whether you deserve it or you don't deserve it – let go of it!"

This is what happens with us: we act a certain way, and the Lord says, "Just let go of it. It doesn't matter." God's love doesn't take notice of those things. God will give it to you. There was one man that we had helped an awful lot, and he was a preacher. We had helped him and got him out of one situation and then another. We prayed him out of it with his family and with all kinds of things. And when he'd talk about me, he'd call me "that woman." "She...that woman," you know. All the years that I helped him, I said, "How long,

Lord am I going to have to help this man and not even get any respect out of him?" He didn't even remember my name, after years and years of helping him.

Well, sometimes these things we have to put up with. But how do we react to it? I just said, "Lord, I think I've helped him long enough." But the Lord didn't feel that way. "But, Lord, I've had enough." One time I said, "Lord, I'm going to put the padlock on the door, and I'm not going to have any more people come ever again." I only said that a couple times to the Lord. But the Lord said, "Now you know you're not going to do that."

God's love is what has to reach out and change hearts. Children's hearts, adult's hearts, everybody's hearts. **God's love has to do it.** We can't do it by beating them, yelling at them or screaming at them. We can't do it by getting angry with them. It does not work that way. Sometimes we feel like it, and sometimes we do it, but it doesn't work.

God's love endures all things.

There comes a time when God says, "That's enough." There have been a few people in my life that God has brought me to them and said, "You don't have any more to do with them. It's finished." Thank God, not too many. But because the Lord said it was enough, we drew back, and those people never went anywhere with God. They went backward, because God knew what was in their hearts. God knew the very things they were doing against Him and against His Spirit and His Word and against His love.

IV. Love Endures Long And Is Patient

The Lord wants to build up in every one of us this love that endures long and is patient. Most people – young people – don't have any patience. But **patience is something you learn by enduring.** And sometimes I hear remarks one to another, and I can tell they're not enduring anything. They are not showing God's love, and they are not enduring anything. But God says His love endures. It's patient. It's kind. We need today to hear His Word and say, "Lord, fill me with Your love. Fill my heart, fill my mind, fill my body with Your love."

It must be precept upon precept, precept upon precept and line upon line, and line upon line, here a little and there a little. **God will change your life.** This is the hardest thing we have to do. Why? He says, "I'm only putting My love in you. So that when you go out to other countries, they're going to know that you've been sent by Me. And that My love is in you, and they are going to respond to My love." Every human being, unless they've turned reprobate or powers of Satan totally control them, is affected by God's love. God is calling us to intercede, to pray, to love one another, to uphold His Word, to show His love even when the situation is unlovely. God is so faithful to us, that we need to be faithful to Him. We need to remember this Word that He's giving to us.

"Finally, brethren, whatsoever things are true, whatsoever things are honest, whatsoever things are just, whatsoever things are pure, whatsoever things are lovely, whatsoever things are of good report; if there be any virtue, if there be any praise, think on these things. Those things which ye have both learned and received and heard and seen in me," Paul said, "...do:" He didn't say, "You hear me say it," did he? Now listen to it: "And heard and **seen** in me..." That is a little more than just hearing it? "...and the God of peace shall be with you." In this place God imparts with every Word that He gives out of this Bible – He imparts it to you.

You have the right to receive it. You have the right to make it your very own, because He's **giving** it to you. So, if you want to come up a little higher in His love, receive it!

He's giving it to you so that you can be like Him. He's giving it to you, because Paul said, "What you have learned and received and heard and seen in me..." Paul was the example that God used to show the people His love and His Word. "That which you have both learned, received and heard and seen in me," Paul said, "...do." "...do and the God of peace shall be with you." He's imparting it to us even now.

Now, I declare unto you He's going to try you. I know so. So "Be ye kind one to another, tenderhearted, forgiving one another, as God for Christ's sake hath forgiven you." Amen? Then love one another with the love of God, and it won't bounce back. We won't become sour or bitter or resentful, but it will flow from Him and from you to others.

When we went into Africa, and into India, God sent us. He had prepared us, so that when we went, we would not be afraid. He prepared us **in His love** that when we went, they would know it was God. We went into cannibal villages, we went into all kinds of villages. We went into a Moslem village, and the man who loaned us His jeep was a Moslem. We went in there ... and the minister with us said, "Well, we won't be here long, because they're Moslem." Do you know what happened? I said, "Lord, You give me the words that are going to touch the hearts of those people." And He did! And they gave their lives to Jesus. They came out of the fields, and they kept coming and they kept coming. There was a man and a woman there, and the Lord told me to give them this Bible and to tell them to nurture and train these people by the Spirit of the Lord. They stood there and tears run down their face, and they said, "We know that's God, because God has put in our hearts to do that for the people." We had to go; we couldn't stay. We don't know what happened, but we do know God put the care of it with someone whom He had appointed to take care of them.

Never once did they say to us, "It isn't God" or "It isn't God's love." They knew it was God's love. They knew that God had sent us. And this is true of our lives; we need to know what we have heard and seen by His love, then Paul says, "...do it." "...do it."

V. The Greatest Of These Is Love

I thank the Lord for what He is doing in every one of our hearts, **we need to press in.** We need to allow His love to take the place of all the other things that we have that are not beneficial to us, or to Him. It won't work. Only God's love is going to work; only His joy is going to work, only His faith operating in us. The greatest of these is His love.

God wants to bring us into that relationship so that we can do the right things when we're dealing with people and dealing with children. So that we don't damage them, but that His love prevails over everything else. I grant you there is an aggravation by the enemy a lot of times, that we would like to do something different. But I believe God is bringing us into a place with Him, that will help us to have understanding and patience with every situation. **God wants to put His love in us and remove the "mixture,"** so that He can make us strong to go out there and win people of any faith or all faiths to Him because He's the One that's going to do it. We just need to let Him do it. Paul said here: "Let your moderation be known unto all men. The Lord is at hand." And if he felt He was at hand, how much more do we know that He is at hand, and that we need God to prepare our hearts so that He can use us in touching other hearts and other lives.

Closing Prayer

Father, we thank You for the Word. We thank You, Lord Jesus, that You made the way for Your perfect love to be in us. God, we thank You that You so loved the world that You gave Jesus to us. And, Jesus, You so loved us, that You died for us. Now, Lord, let us so love You that Your love will saturate our hearts, our minds, our entire being. Impart Your love to us, Jesus. Let all these other things pass away. But let Your love remain in our hearts and in our minds. We thank You, Lord Jesus, for Your Word, but we thank You for what You have done to bring it to pass that we might have this love abiding in us.

That we might reach out to the unlovely, the uncared for, those who don't have anybody to love them or to care for them. God, teach us Your ways that we may walk in them, and that we might fulfill Your Word according to Your Word and according to Your Spirit. Jesus, we thank

You for this Word. Let it sink into our hearts. Let us move by it, Jesus. Let us desire more than anything to let Your love fill every part of our being until others can see Jesus in us. Lord, we thank You for this Word. Let it penetrate to the depths of our being, Lord, and cause us to respond with Your love, that we might love one another.

Bless this people, each and every one that's here. Let Your love penetrate into them, and let these other things pass away. But let Your love remain, Jesus. Let Your peace remain. Let Your joy remain, Lord, that our joy may be full. We thank You for this Word . Jesus, we praise You now for the impartation by Your Spirit of Your love, Your peace, Your joy, Your righteousness and Your holiness, Lord.

Make us to be Your people that desire You more than anything in this world, that You might use us to bring the world to Jesus. Jesus, we thank You for this precious Word that You've imparted to us. We thank You for the growth by Your Spirit, Lord, according to Your Word. We give You glory now, Jesus, and we praise You for everything You have done and are now doing, and we thank You for the finished work of Your great love. In Your Name, Jesus, we ask it, and for Your glory. Amen.

REVIEW: COME UP HIGHER IN HIS LOVE

True or False

1. ___ God wants to so transform our lives with His love that we do not have the interference of human love – realizing that God's love surpasses
2. anything else.
3. ___ Human love mixed with God's love is perfect.
4. ___ God wants to remove carnal love, and put a love for others that we will not be affected by circumstances.
5. ___ Love bears up under almost anything and everything that comes.
6. ___ We are living in the hour of the Spirit of Truth.
7. ___ God's love is worked in our lives by processing.
8. ___ What God is doing in our life is forever.

9. ___ If we're trained to go out to other countries, it's very, very important that we are trained in the little things.
10. ___ God wants His love to take the place of human love, which is selfish, self-centered, self-seeking, jealous, vainglorious, boastful, and haughty.
11. ___ Sometimes fits of anger exemplify the love of God.
12. ___ All it takes is determination to let the Lord change our lives.
13. ___ Sometimes even God's love wants something in return.
14. ___ God wants His love to have charge of our life. But it's up to us.
15. ___ God's love is pure.
16. ___ Love bears up under anything and everything that comes; is ever ready to believe the best of every person, its hopes are fadeless under all circumstances and it endures everything (without weakening).
17. ___ Patience is something you learn by enduring.
18. ___ God is calling us to intercede, to pray, to love one another, to uphold His Word, to show His love even when a situation is unlovely.
19. ___ We need to allow His love to take the place of all other things that we have that are not beneficial to us or to Him.
20. ___ God wants to put His love in us and remove the "mixture," so that He can make us strong to go and win people of any faith or all faiths to Him.

21. ___ God is bringing us into a place with Him that will help us to have understanding and patience with every situation.
22. ___ "Those things , which ye have both learned and received and heard and seen in me, do: and the God of peace shall be with you."
23. ___ You don't have the right to receive the impartation of God's Word.
24. ___ God will do it all; we don't need to press in.
25. ___ God is faithful to us, but we don't really need to be faithful to Him.
26. ___ God will prepare us, so that when He sends us, we will not be afraid.

CHAPTER 13
WHERE TO FIND A WORD?

Building Block Series: Where Do we Find a Word? – Are you Called or Did You Go?

Are You Called?

EVERY ONE OF us who love and serve God are called to a purpose. We were given special talents and abilities that we need to fulfill His plan for our lives. Each of us is unique. Some love the details and others love the grand story. A few are gifted athletically and others excel in music. There are those who love to read and those who would rather take a walk in nature. **We are all created with a special purpose in mind.**

Psalm 139:13-18 New Life Version (NLV)

13 For You made the parts inside me. You put me together inside my mother. 14 I will give thanks to You, for the greatness of the way I was made brings fear. Your works

are great and my soul knows it very well. 15 My bones were not hidden from You when I was made in secret and put together with care in the deep part of the earth. 16 Your eyes saw me before I was put together. And all the days of my life were written in Your book before any of them came to be. 17 Your thoughts are of great worth to me, O God. How many there are!

The Prophet, Jeremiah, was called from his mother's womb (Jeremiah 1:5)

Paul said God had, "separated me from my mother's womb" (Galatians 1:15)

Others, such as Isaiah, had a specific time that God called them. For example; Abraham, Gideon, Ezekiel and others. We might have a sense that we are called by God from when we are young, or it might come as a total surprise.

Romans 10:15 And how shall they preach, **except they be sent?** as it is written, How beautiful are the feet of them that preach the gospel of peace, and bring glad tidings of good things!

Don't think that your calling has to do with your qualifications, abilities, achievements or even your walk with God. You are called by Him and you are formed for His purpose. **Finding His purpose for you is the difference between striving in your own strength and flowing by His Spirit.** You will find the greatest fruitfulness and fulfillment when you "abide in the vine" and draw the source of your strength and guidance from Him. When you stay in what He has called you to do and move in His anointing you will find yourself flowing by His Spirit.

. . .

LET'S REVIEW - *ARE YOU CALLED?*

Where Do I Find a Word?

The word of God is **something which comes from Him** and not from our own mind. Our minds are constantly being fed by what we have heard and what we are thinking. It is what He is speaking about a situation which is really important. We are often affected by circumstances and our reactions to them. We can be easily swayed by people and what they say and think. But, if we allow God to train us we can **learn to hear His voice and sense His heart.** If we stay close to Him and develop a relationship with Him we can begin to hear clearly and consistently.

Here are some things we can do to cooperate with the Holy Spirit who is preparing us to faithfully be His "Mouthpiece".

- Keep Refreshed. Building yourself up in your most Holy Faith. Jude 1:20-25
- Have **your own** quiet time.
- Pray, intercede, worship, study, meditate, journal and fellowship with God.

Prayer is talking with your Father and listening for His responses. It is presenting your requests, needs and challenges and also sharing your joys and thanks. Philippians 4:6 Do not be anxious about anything. Instead, in every situation, through prayer and petition with thanksgiving, tell your requests to God.

To intercede is to stand in the gap between God and His people. It is praying by the Holy Spirit according to God's will for His people. When we pray by the Holy Spirit, often we will feel His heart and weep for what makes Him weep.

Romans 8:26 In the same way, the Spirit helps us in our weakness, for we do not know how we should pray, but the Spirit himself intercedes for us with inexpressible groanings.

To worship is to allow your whole being to express how great, awesome, amazing, kind, precious, righteous, just and lovely He is. He meets us in worship. Worship helps remind us how loving and great is our God and put our needs in perspective.

To study is to look deeply into God's word; Comparing scripture with scripture.

To meditate is to focus on some truth or attribute of God and prayerfully consider that area of truth.

To journal is to write your prayer requests, anything God speaks to you, verses which become meaningful and thoughts which come to you while meditating.

To fellowship with God is to practice His presence in your life no matter what you are doing and what is happening around you can still be aware of Him. Share every need, every joy and every concern. Be listening for His voice and be sensitive to His Spirit's nudge.

Let's Review - *Where do I Find a Word?*

How to Study the Word of God

As you spend time in God's word for yourself you will be filled and changed and you will have more inside of you to give to others.

Study by Subject. ie: The Basics of Salvation or Water Baptism etc.

Chronological. The history and order of events.

Study verse by verse through the Bible.

Study People. Character studies or Bible Places can also be very interesting.

Word Studies. Meanings and definitions can help us better understand Truth if we allow the Holy Spirit to minister to us and lead us in better understanding

Revelation. Often God will open our hearts to receive and understand something which we were blind to previously but now we see. When this is happening it is a great time to find this truth in scripture.

Inspiration: This is where God's Word encourages and lifts you up and will help you get through difficult times and help you work with challenging people with His grace.

Promises. There are thousands of promises in the Bible and they are all for us to stand on. Most of the promises have an "if". When we look for the "if" and fulfill it God will do His part.

Strengthen your Faith and find encouragement. Just one phrase in a verse can be enough to lift your heart above the difficulties.

Guidance. The principles are everywhere in the Bible. When we apply them we will prosper and be successful in what we are doing.

Social Issues and current events. Study what Gods word says about social issues. Times change and people change but God's word will stand forever. There is always an answer to the situations people face that can be found in

His word. When we direct people to what God says we will be standing on His Rock.

Let's Review - *How to Study the Word of God*

Three Kinds of People.

Every servant of God needs three kinds of people in their lives.

We all need people. No minister is all sufficient or an island. Ministers also need to be ministered to. We all need encouragement, deliverance and accountability. Yes, ministering to others by the flow of God's Spirit also brings refreshing to us; but, to keep ourselves balanced, we need other people; difficult people, happy people, friendly ones and challenging ones.

Three Kinds of People. We should have **disciples**, we need to be **discipled** and we need **fellowship**.

It is very important that we know God and understand His word. But we must also relate well to people. Many ministers become imbalanced in their life if they do not have healthy relationships with their families, friends, colleagues and their sheep. **There are probably more splits in church bodies caused by personal differences than by essential doctrinal issues.** Let us excel in loving people.

Let's look at the three different kinds of relationships that will help us keep balanced.

People we are ministering to. Young ones cannot just grow up on their own. They need someone to take them, lead them and disciple them. This does not mean just in Bible Study but in all of life. People will grow best when they have a Spiritual Mother or Father. **Young disciples**

will challenge our faith and examine our walk. They are good for our "health". They will keep us young and flexible.

People who are our equals, our friends, who we can be ourselves with and who can reflect back to us how they see us. When we are "just being ourselves" are we still godly? Our **friends will see a different side of us than our sheep**. It is not healthy for anyone to be in the role of pastor or leader all of the time. Having health relationships with friends will help us keep spiritually natural and naturally spiritual.

People who mentor us and keep us accountable. Those who can call us and correct us when we are off track. Those who are ministering to us and feeding us. Prophets, Teachers, Intercessors and Apostles.

Our culture may not understand the principle of discipleship and apprenticeship that was common at the time Jesus was on earth. When Jesus called his disciples they **felt that it was a great honor** to be chosen by a "Teacher or Rabbi" to be trained to become "as his teacher". Even the family members would rejoice that one of their family was chosen.

So many things that we learn in life are "caught more than taught". It is while we go through challenges together with another person that we learn the best. **Hands on training will help us more than classroom teaching.** We have many teachers, but not many "Fathers". Paul said, "I have begotten you through the gospel."

1Corinthians 4:15 For though ye have ten thousand instructors in Christ, yet have ye not many fathers: for in Christ Jesus I have begotten you through the gospel.

We will be very blessed when we find spiritual Fathers

or Mothers who will "watch for our souls" and speak into our lives. **Intentionally seek out this kind of relationship** in your ministry.

Let's Review - *Three Kinds of People*

REVIEW: WHERE TO FIND A WORD?

Are You Called?

1. List 10 Special abilities God has blessed you with.
2. Have you been given prophetic words about your calling? Write a summary of what you have received.
3. What Godly area or activity is the most interesting to you. Which type of Godly people do you follow and admire. Which character in the Bible would you most want to be like?

Where do I Find a Word?

1. List which of the quiet time activities do you already consistently use?
2. Pick a new activity from the lesson to add to your time with God. Write a plan to begin adding this new idea to your quiet times.

3. Do you sense yourself growing closer to God? What steps do you plan to make to draw nearer to Him?

4. Choose one scripture which has been meaningful to you recently and write what this verse has meant to you.

How to Study the Word of God

1. Read Psalm 119. List how many different ways you find that David interacts with the Word of God?

2. Choose a new method you have not used before and explain how you plan to include this in your Bible studies.

Three Kinds of People

1. Look at your own life, list people that you have in each of the three areas of relationship. If you have an empty area make a plan and write it out.

2. Explain what it means when Paul says, "I have begotten you through the gospel"

3. Explain what it means to disciple someone.

QUIZ: WHERE TO FIND A WORD

1. When you stay in what He has called you to do and move in His anointing you will find yourself flowing by His Spirit.
a. T
b. F

2. God calls us because of our special abilities, our qualifications and our walk with Him
a. T
b. F

3. We can begin to hear God's voice clearly and consistently as we
a. Listen to quiet worship music
b. Develop a close relationship with Him
c. Constantly feed our minds by what we hear and what we are thinking
d. None of the above

4. As we intercede by the Holy Spirit we might begin to weep for what makes Him weep
a. T
b. F

5. Meditating on God means:
a. Sitting with your legs crossed thinking about nothing
b. Emptying yourself of all of your own thoughts and feelings
c. To focus on some truth or attribute of God and prayerfully consider that area of truth
d. All of the above

6. Fellowshipping with God is:
a. To practice His presence in every part of your life
b. To share every joy and concern with God
c. To be sensitive to His gentle voice throughout your day
d. All of the above

7. When our hearts are open to understand something we were blind to is called
a. Inspiration
b. Fellowship
c. Intercession
d. Revelation

8. When God's Word encourages us and helps us deal with a difficult person or circumstance this is called
a. Intercession
b. Inspiration
c. Fellowship

d. Revelation

9. Everyone needs to have 3 kinds of people in their lives to keep well balanced
a. The good, the bad and the ugly
b. Sheep, goats and donkeys
c. Mentors, disciples and fellowship

10. Young disciples need us but will also keep us young and flexible
a. T
b. F

11. People who are our equals can help us stay naturally spiritual and spiritually natural
a. T
b. F

12. Hands on training is not as valuable as classroom study
a. T
b. F

13. We have many Fathers but not many teachers
a. T
b. F

14. You may have to intentionally seek out and pursue a mentor
a. T
b. F

15. The Word you give flows out of the Word you live
a. T
b. F

CHAPTER 14
DO THEY KNOW YOU?

So you want to be a Pastor? **But do your sheep know you?**

Jesus is the Good Shepherd.

As leaders we must learn His ways and learn to love His people as if the flock is His not ours. As we minister and demonstrate God's love for His flock they will begin to know us and love us. As trust, love and respect develop we can impart God's sheep the wisdom and lessons that God gives us from His throne.

In John 10 Jesus shares how He is the Good Shepherd and how His sheep know His voice. He also shares how we can **follow His example as good shepherds.**

John 10:4 And when he putteth forth his own sheep, he goeth before them, and the sheep follow him: for they know his voice.

When a shepherd feeds his sheep and cares for them they know him. If someone else calls them the sheep will ignore them or run away. But when the shepherd calls the sheep come to him and follow him.

If a sheep is hungry, the shepherd feeds him, thirsty, he gives him something to drink, if he is sick, the shepherd cares for him until he is well.

Jesus is the Good Shepherd here are some examples of how He takes care of us as sheep. The **Good Shepherd is concerned for our needs** our physical needs like food and clothing as well as our spiritual needs.

Psalm 23:1 The LORD [is] my shepherd; I shall not want. 2 He maketh me to lie down in green pastures: he leadeth me beside the still waters.

Isaiah 58:6 [Is] not this the fast that I have chosen? to loose the bands of wickedness, to undo the heavy burdens, and to let the oppressed go free, and that ye break every yoke? 7 [Is it] not to deal thy bread to the hungry, and that thou bring the poor that are cast out to thy house? when thou seest the naked, that thou cover him; and that thou hide not thyself from thine own flesh?

Let us ask ourselves these questions:
Why do I have a church?
Personal fulfillment, ego, arrogance.
Just to say I have a church.
Just to fulfill my call.
Just for income.
Because God called me.
Because I love people and I love working with them.
Does your congregation trust You?
Do they know you have their best interest in mind?

Many times people enter into a role as a pastor or leader and do not think of the practical ways that they will "Feed their Sheep". Do we understand that it is our responsibility to feed and water the sheep and bring the sheep into a place where they can reproduce.

As Pastors we prepare our sheep.

To Live:

- Basic Foundation
- Repentance
- Salvation
- Water Baptism
- Baptism of the Holy Ghost
- Use the Word appropriately
- Grow Spiritually
- Develop the Fruit of the Spirit
- Move by the Spirit of the Lord
- Administer the sacraments *(Biblical ceremonies)*
- Communion

- Tithes and Offering
- Water Baptism
- Wash each others feet
- Memorize the Word

To Reproduce:

- Sunday schools - Foundational teaching
- Youth groups
- Teach how to tell others about Jesus
- Weddings
- Baby dedications
- Training leaders
- Reproduce God.... His kingdom

For Loss:

- Illnesses
- Hospital
- Disasters
- Persecution
- Loss of loved one

For Leadership:

- Usher
- Deacon
- Administrator
- Minister

- Pastor
- Teacher
- Evangelist
- Apostle

As Pastors we **nurture the believer into maturity,** helping them to fulfill their calling by the Spirit of the Lord. We train our congregation how to enter into the rest of the Lord and to live in peace. We continually offer prayer and intercession for our sheep.

Psalm 23:3 He restoreth my soul: he leadeth me in the paths of righteousness for his name's sake.

Philippians 4:9 Those things, which ye have both learned, and received, and heard, and seen in me, do: and the God of peace shall be with you.

Our responsibility is not to keep our congregation inside the church but to nurture them and **train them to go into all of the world.**

Paul's Example of a Good Shepherd:

2 Timothy 2:24 And the servant of the Lord must not strive; but be gentle unto all men, apt to teach, patient, 25 In meekness instructing those that oppose themselves; if God peradventure will give them repentance to the acknowledging of the truth; 26 And that they may recover themselves out of the snare of the devil, who are taken captive by him at his will.

Gal 4:19 My little children, of whom I **travail in birth again** until Christ be formed in you,

Let's read Matthew 25:34-40

34 "Then the King will say to those on His right side, 'Come, you who have been called by My Father. Come into the holy nation that has been made ready for you before the world was made. 35 For I was hungry and you gave Me food to eat. I was thirsty and you gave Me water to drink. I was a stranger and you gave Me a room. 36 I had no clothes and you gave Me clothes to wear. I was sick and you cared for Me. I was in prison and you came to see Me.'

37 "Then those that are right with God will say, 'Lord, when did we see You hungry and feed You? When did we see You thirsty and give You a drink? 38 When did we see You a stranger and give You a room? When did we see You had no clothes and we gave You clothes? 39 And when did we see You sick or in prison and we came to You?' 40 Then the King will say, 'For sure, I tell you, because you did it to one of the least of My brothers, you have done it to Me.'

We visit our congregation when they are in the hospital, spend time with them during happy and sad life events. Eat meals, pray, serve and teach them **showing that you care.**

Truly, He is the Good Shepherd and we are responsible to care for His sheep and we must always remember - **only Sheep can give birth to sheep**

REVIEW: DO THEY KNOW YOU

1. As a Pastor it is important to learn God's ways and learn to love His people.
a. True
b. False

2. The Good Shepherd is concerned for our needs our physical needs like food and clothing as well as our spiritual needs.
a. True
b. False

3. Why should a pastor have a church? (Choose all that are correct)
a. Personal fulfillment, ego, arrogance.
b. Because God called him.
c. Just to say he has a church.
d. Because he loves people
e. Just to fulfill his call.
f. Just for income.

g. Because he loves working with people.

4. Does your congregation _____ You? Do they know you have their _____ _____ in mind?

5. It is not the concern of the pastor to help those in his church to fulfill their calling by the Spirit of the Lord.
a. True
b. False

6. We continually offer prayer and intercession for our sheep.
a. True
b. False

7. What are 5 ways to show your congregation that you care.
a. Play golf when they are in the hospital
b. Attend their children's weddings
c. Have events at the church that they will enjoy
d. Visit their family members in jail.
e. Do not invite them to your home
f. Pray for their needs in Sunday service
g. Serve them at the church BBQ

8. It is good to train your congregation in the following ways (choose one)
a. Sunday schools - Foundational teaching
b. Youth groups
c. Teach how to tell others about Jesus
d. Training leaders

e. Reproduce God.... His kingdom
f. All of the above

9. A pastor or leader and should only think of spiritual ways to minister to his church.
a. True
b. False

10. Only sheep give birth to sheep means that the church will grow when they are spiritually healthy.
a. True
b. False

KEYS

1. Allowing God's Perfect Peace

1. Righteous, truth
2. perfect peace, mind, trusteth
3. strength
4. judgments, righteousness
5. peace
6. transformed, renewing
7. light, fellowship, cleanseth

True or False
1. T
2. T
3. T
4. T
5. F
6. T

7. T
8. T
9. T
10. T
11. T
12. T
13. T
14. T

Matching
1. b.
2. a.
3. c.
4. f.
5. d.
6. e.
7. g.
8. h.
9. j.
10. i.
11. k.
12. l.

2. Attitude or Altitude

1. b
2. True
3. c
4. False

5. e
6. d
7. a, c, d, f, h
8. teach, seduce, my, servants, fornication
9. T

3. Lord, You Have Ordained Peace for Us

1 b
2 c
3 a
4 c
5 b
6 a
7 b
8 c
9 a
10 b

4. Spiritual Warfare

1 a
2 b
3 a
4 b
5 b
6 a
7 d
8 b

10 d
11 a
12 a
13 d
14 b
15 b

5. Conflict Revolution

1. b
2. a
3. a
4. a
5. b
6. b, c, d
7. c
8. b
9. a
10. b
11. b
12. b, c, d, g
13. f
14. b, c, f, g
15. c
16. d

6. Of No Reputation

True or False
1. F

2. T
3. F
4. F
5. F
6. T
7. T
8. T
9. F
10. T
11. T
12. F
13. T
14. T
15. T
16. T
17. T
18. T
19. T
20. T

7. Shepherds and Sheep

1. a, b, c, e, g, k
2. False
3. a
4. c
5. True
6. a, d, e, h, i, j, l
7. c

8. Faith Worketh By Love

1. Liberty
2. Righteous
3. Love
4. Law
5. Flesh
6. Determination
7. Christ Jesus
8. Water Baptized
9. Creature
10. Walk
11. Spiritual
12. Change
13. Training

True or False
14. F
15. T
16. F

Multiple Choice
17. c.
18. b.
19. c.
20. a.

9. Plumbline

1. plumbline, plumbline, plumbline, people

2. Lord, commitment, total surrender
3. joy, salvation, love, trust
4. Choices, live
5. True
6. allow, willing, liberty, righteousness
7. outlet, kindness, serving, needs, gospels, did, requires

10. The Vision Statement

1. a
2. b
3. a
4. d
5. b
6. b
7. a
8. a
9. d
10. a

11. Praise and Worship

1. True
2. False
3. True
4. Guard, presence, healing, restoration
5. Pure, heart, shame
6. Yes
7. True
8. False

9. Chose, strengthens
10. b
11. d
12. c
13. Compliment, expect, assist
14. b

12. Come Up Higher In His Love

True or False

1. T
2. F
3. T
4. F
5. T
6. T
7. T
8. T
9. T
10. F
11. T
12. F
13. T
14. T
15. T
16. T
17. T
18. T
19. T
20. T

21. T
22. F
23. F
24. F
25. T

13. Where to Find a Word?

1. a
2. b
3. b
4. a
5. c
6. d
7. d
8. b
9. c
10. a
11. a
12. b
13. b
14. a
15. a

14. Do They Know You?

1. True
2. concerned, physical, spiritual
3. b, d, g
4. trust, best, interest

5. False
6. True
7. b, c, d, f, g
8. f
9. False
10. True

ACKNOWLEDGMENTS

Thank you to those who have:

"I planted the seed. Apollos watered it, but it was God Who kept it growing." 1 Corinthians 3:6-8 (NLV)
Thank You

Isaiah 58 Mobile Training Institute website:
is58mti.org

www.ingramcontent.com/pod-product-compliance
Lightning Source LLC
Chambersburg PA
CBHW071307110526
44591CB00010B/804